A HOLY
MEAL

A HOLY MEAL

The Lord's Supper in the Life of the Church

GORDON T. SMITH

B

Baker Academic

Grand Rapids, Michigan

© 2005 by Gordon T. Smith

Published by Baker Academic
a division of Baker Publishing Group
P.O. Box 6287, Grand Rapids, MI 49516-6287
www.bakeracademic.com

Printed in the United States of America

                Library of Congress Cataloging-in-Publication Data
Smith, Gordon T., 1953–
    A holy meal : the Lord's Supper in the life of the church / Gordon T.
Smith.
         p.   cm.
    Includes bibliographical references and index.
    ISBN 0-8010-2768-3
    1. Lord's Supper. I. Title.
BV825.3.S65 2005
234'.163—dc22   2004029536

CONTENTS

PART 1

Eating, Symbol, and Sacrament

1

EATING AND THE REIGN OF GOD

We cannot live without eating. Even more remarkable, eating is a spiritual practice. We are reminded by the testimony of Scripture and the spiritual heritage of the church that eating and drinking are not merely responses to physical hunger. While the acts of eating and drinking do meet our physical needs, in them something else also happens that satisfies the deepest longings of our souls.

The study that follows considers the meal of the church—the holy meal that is traditionally known as Holy Communion, the Eucharist, or the Lord's Supper. On the one hand, this meal involves an intentional encounter with God. This holy meal profiles the relationship of the Christian church to a Triune God and is also a means by which God is experienced as Father, Son, and Spirit. The Lord's Supper is also a meal in which we celebrate the reign of God and communicate that we are a people who live in this reign. In other words, this is a meal that enables us to live those dimensions of life that matter most. Indeed, one might easily conclude that in this meal the critical contours of the spiritual life are both delineated and maintained. The encounter with the risen, ascended Lord Jesus Christ enables the church to live in the world but as participants in the reign of God. We are in but not of the world.

Both of these—the relationship with God through the ascended Christ and the way of being in the world while under the rule of God—are effected in our lives through the work of the Spirit. What we ask for when we pray for the gift of the Spirit is known and experienced in the holy meal. Or to put it differently, when we ask for the Spirit, what we long for is precisely what is offered to us in the Lord's Supper.

Therefore, the *epiclesis*—the ancient prayer for the coming of the Spirit—is not a petition that merely supplements or complements our celebration of the Lord's Supper; this prayer is the heart of the matter. We participate in the Lord's Supper *in the Spirit,* and as we leave, we pray that we will return to the world in the fullness of the Spirit. What needs to be emphasized is that it is precisely in the actual celebration of this sacred event that we experience the very grace for which we long when we pray, "Oh, come, Spirit of God." Each dimension of meaning in the Lord's Supper—each grace received—is but another facet of the gift that is given to the church through the ministry of the Spirit. This study of the Lord's Supper is, then, a consideration of the ministry of the Spirit as it is manifested in the life of the community of faith. This gift is, in the end, the grace to live under the liberating reign of Christ.

There is another recurring theme in this study of the Lord's Supper: The holy meal is a communal event; it is about eating *together.* The encounter with the ascended Christ and the experience of the grace of the Spirit's ministry are experienced *together.* We live in a time of increasing emphasis on individual sensibilities and needs, what essentially has become a spirituality of the personal self. There is some legitimacy to this. We need solitude; it is a necessary part of the life and practices of a maturing Christian. We need to learn how to make choices, to act with courage, and to develop as mature persons. We need to know ourselves, as individuals, and to know what matters to us, what it is that we are called to do, and to have the courage to do this without caving in to the demands and expectations of others. Yet this can easily descend into personal autonomy. We can so easily come to feel that we need no one. Our social context encourages us to make our own choices, live our own lives, and engage with

10

others only when we think they have something to offer us. This is not a Christian spirituality. Further, it is an approach to life that does not foster true engagement with God or truly enable us to experience the full grace of being a Christian. The words of 1 John 1:3–4 remind us that joy is made complete when we are in fellowship with God and one another. Nothing so enables this as the Lord's Supper. Nothing so effectively mitigates against the propensity toward individual autonomy within our culture and within Western Christianity as the Lord's Supper. This meal is a means by which we see, feel, and taste that we are in this together. We need one another. We depend on one another. Together we will know God and grow in faith, hope, and love.

We can certainly read the Bible together and serve together and participate in a number of activities that enable us to experience God together, but nothing quite like the Lord's Supper so enables us to declare *and* experience our common faith.

Eating and the Old Covenant

The genius of the event is that it is a meal—a holy meal, but a meal nevertheless. We appreciate its significance all the more when we recognize that the meal is a central motif in the Bible, particularly in connection with God's salvation. The biblical story begins with food: The first human parents were invited to eat, with the proviso that their eating was to be an expression of thankfulness, obedience, and dependence on God. Alas, it was in their eating that they chose to disobey.

It comes as no surprise, then, that eating plays such a crucial role in the inauguration of the Old Testament covenant. Because the parents of humanity ate in disobedience, it is appropriate that the covenant God graciously established with their descendants, notably the children of Abraham and Sarah, was set in place around a meal. This covenant feast was marked by thankfulness, obedience, and dependence on the provision of God. The fellowship of the meal happened in the *presence* of God.

> Then Moses and Aaron, Nadab, and Abihu, and seventy of the elders of Israel went up, and they saw the God of Israel. Under his feet there was something like a pavement of sapphire stone,

11

like the very heaven for clearness. God did not lay his hand on
the chief men of the people of Israel; also they beheld God, and
they ate and drank.

Exodus 24:9–11

Then in describing the sacrificial system, the book of Leviticus
makes regular references to the act of eating in connection with
the sacrifices. Some of the sacrifices were burnt up completely,
it would seem, but while the peace offering was presented to
God, it was then actually consumed by the worshiper, specifically and intentionally in the presence of God. It is significant
that the potential reasons for celebrating a peace offering, as
described in Leviticus 7:12, also find expression in our celebration of the Lord's Supper: A peace offering could be given as an
act of thanksgiving, it could serve as an occasion to renew the
covenant, or it could be a celebration of God's goodness and
providential care.

Mention also needs to be made of the extraordinary down-
pour of the manna—the bread from heaven. This was clearly a
physical and tangible act of God, a means by which God's people
ate, were nourished, and lived. But it was so much more. The
people of Israel were regularly reminded that this was a daily
provision; it was a manifest demonstration of their complete
dependence on God's providential care. But what makes this
doubly fascinating is that immediately prior to the coming of
Jesus, the teachers of Israel spoke of the Messiah, who would
bring down a new manna. Then Jesus came and, as we read in
John 6, spoke of himself as this bread from heaven.

The wisdom literature of the Old Testament contains some
intriguing references to eating and drinking. Sometimes the
eating of the wise speaks of divine blessing. At other times, it
is an expression of the height and joy of wisdom, such as when
we read, "Come, eat of my bread and drink of the wine I have
mixed. Lay aside immaturity, and live, and walk in the way of
insight" (Prov. 9:5). Here eating is portrayed as an intentional
act of response to the call of *sophia*, the call to wisdom.

Then in the Prophets, we find this call:

Ho, everyone who thirsts,
  come to the waters;

and you that have no money,
    come, buy and eat!
Come, buy wine and milk
    without money and without price.
Why do you spend your money for that which is not bread,
    and your labor for that which does not satisfy?
Listen carefully to me, and eat what is good,
    and delight yourselves in rich food.
Incline your ear, and come to me;
    listen, so that you may live.

Isaiah 55:1–3

Here, and earlier in Isaiah (25:6–9), we see that the future of Israel is to be one of plenty and that this plenty will be experienced in festive eating and drinking. But this eschatological vision is complemented by a call to the present. Since the future is secure, the prophet urges the people to live accordingly and to anticipate and seek that which is consistent with the life to come. In this remarkable interconnection between listening and eating, eating and drinking represent the deepest yearnings of the soul—longings that can, in the end, be fulfilled only by God. There is also a hint of something significant here: We only eat well, in the kingdom, when we *listen* well. Conversely, it appears that we only truly listen when we eat "what is good." Listening and eating go together.

Eating and the Ministry of Jesus

Given this backdrop in the Old Testament, it is no surprise that the New Testament reveals that eating was important for Jesus and that the new covenant was both inaugurated and renewed around a meal—the Lord's Supper. But the Last Supper was only one of the many meals Jesus ate. Eating was for Jesus a key means by which he proclaimed the coming of God's reign and acted, or *enacted*, its arrival. Meals were a central way in which Jesus portrayed the values and vision of the covenant and the meaning of the rule of God. He often referred to eating and drinking in the kingdom of God, and in speaking to his disciples, he anticipated that day when he would eat and drink with them "at my table in my kingdom" (Luke 22:30).

Jesus ate with his followers, with his friends, and with outcasts. It was so much a part of his ministry and his life that one almost gets the sense that when he wasn't preaching and teaching he was eating. In so doing, he was identifying with the ancient Jewish practice of meal fellowship.[1]

His meals were acts of compassion. He saw and met hungry people, and he fed them. Jesus responded to their most basic needs while always insisting that their fundamental needs were greater than those represented by their immediate physical hunger.

These meals were also acts of acceptance, forgiveness, and mercy. Meal fellowship for the Jewish community was a sign of thanksgiving to a gracious Creator and Redeemer, but it was also a sign of community and fellowship, indeed, of reconciliation. Jesus intentionally ate with those on the margins: outcasts, tax collectors, and those like Zacchaeus and Mary Magdalene, whom others rejected and despised. He welcomed them at a meal. This was scandalous for the religious authorities of the day, but for Jesus, eating with "sinners" was something that necessarily accompanied his preaching and teaching. As Wolfhart Pannenberg

---

1. For much of this section, I am indebted to Geoffrey Wainwright in *Eucharist and Eschatology* (New York: Oxford University Press, 1981), where he argues that there is a direct link between the Eucharist and the meals of Jesus' ministry. In the feeding of the crowds in Mark 6 and 8, he notes the parallels with the action of blessing/thanksgiving, breaking, and distribution that we have in the Last Supper. The feeding of the crowds was a demonstration of God's blessing on all, demonstrated specifically through the offering of food (bread in particular). Wainwright concludes that the Synoptic evangelists clearly described the actions of Jesus at these events through the lens of the Eucharist and as a way to foreshadow the Eucharist. He writes, "The accounts of the feeding miracles are such as to prove that for the primitive church at least, the Eucharist and the miraculous feedings stood in close relation" (35). Wainwright builds his case on the description of the actions and language of Jesus that closely paralleled the action and language of the Lord's Supper. For example, in Matthew 14:19, we read that Jesus took bread, looked to heaven and gave thanks, blessed the bread, broke the bread, and then gave the bread to his disciples and the crowd. The crowd and the disciples ate. Some have suggested that the distribution of the fish is intentionally not mentioned because the point of the evangelists is to highlight the eucharistic link to these feeding miracles.

puts it, "We have in these meals the central symbolic action of Jesus in which his message of the nearness of God's reign and its salvation is focussed and vividly depicted. . . . Everything that separates from God is removed in the table fellowship that Jesus practised."[2]

Then, of course, Jesus ate with his disciples. The Last Supper was the last of many meals Jesus had with them. They felt the weight of the occasion as he told them that this would be his last meal, for the time being, until he would drink with them from the cup in the coming of the kingdom (Matt. 26:29; Mark 14:25; Luke 22:16, 18).

Then Jesus continued to eat with his disciples following the resurrection. He kept meeting them at mealtimes! There is the dramatic encounter in Emmaus, where Jesus was recognized "in the breaking of the bread" (Luke 24:28–35); the meal on Easter Sunday evening, back in Jerusalem (Luke 24:36–43); and the heartwarming encounter between Jesus and the seven disciples who had gone fishing when Jesus himself prepared the meal (John 21:1–14). All of this is so noteworthy that after the ascension Peter witnessed before Cornelius that Jesus "ate and drank" with them after he rose from the dead (Acts 10:41). Indeed, the post-resurrection meals put the "last" supper into a whole new perspective for the disciples. There is a sense in which it made sense to them only in light of the meals they celebrated in the company of the risen Christ. Even after the ascension, then, the early church continued to "break bread" as a celebration of the presence of the risen Christ in their midst (Acts 2:42).

Jesus not only ate but also incorporated meals into his stories. The parable of the lost son, for example, includes a grand celebration at a meal. In so doing, Jesus illustrated something central to his message of the kingdom of God: A messianic meal will be the central event profiled in the coming of that kingdom. Indeed, the hope of Israel was captured in the image of a meal—specifically, a meal when people will come from east and west. This hope was not only for the house of Israel; it clearly incorporated Gentiles as well (Matt. 8:11; Luke 13:29). It is clear that Jesus

---

2. Wolfhart Pannenberg, *Systematic Theology*, vol. 3, trans. Geoffrey W. Bromiley (Grand Rapids: Eerdmans, 1998), 286.

viewed his meals with his disciples as events that anticipated this meal at the consummation of history.

So it comes as no surprise that the early church ate together. Yes, of course, they ate together because Jesus urged them to "do this in remembrance of me." Yet the practice of this meal was also at the heart of their relationship with Jesus. Though Jesus was physically absent, having ascended into heaven, he was mystically present to them at these meals. They fully embraced the words of Revelation 3:20 that if they invited him into their presence and company, he would come in and would eat with them. But they knew that this eating was an act of faith and anticipation as they looked forward to the day when Jesus would be tangibly and physically present to the community of faith. This event in the life of the church, the physical act of eating and drinking, was fundamentally a spiritual event. While it was certainly physical eating and drinking that set the stage for the Lord's Supper, it was in the end a symbolic event. Yes, the church did eat and drink, but what was fulfilled were the deepest yearnings of the human soul, that Jesus would enter in and eat with his people.

This is the joy of the new kingdom. The risen, ascended Christ, the head of the church, responds to the yearnings of a spiritually hungry people. His people take the words of Isaiah 55 to heart when they are asked, "Why do you . . . labor for that which does not satisfy?" (v. 2). They want to respond to the exhortation, "Listen carefully to me, and eat what is good" (v. 2). They do this in a holy meal, the Lord's Supper. As Alexander Schmemann has observed, the original sin of Genesis 3 is not so much that Adam and Eve acted willfully but that they were no longer hungry for God and looking to God for "life."[3] Their eating was a violation of life because they ate in disobedience but also because they ignored God in their eating. Human eating is only truly life giving if it is an expression of gratitude and obedience to God, an eating wherein God is both acknowledged and obeyed.

It is amazing that our salvation is symbolized in an act of eating and drinking. In the event of a meal, we together look back to the failure of our human parents, and we look forward to an

---

3. Alexander Schmemann, *For the Life of the World: Sacraments and Orthodoxy* (Crestwood, NY: St. Vladimir's Seminary Press, 1998), 18.

eating and drinking that will be part of the kingdom that is yet to come. We also eat, very intentionally, as an act of obedience ("Do this in remembrance of me"). By this act we identify with what matters to us most—to live in grateful obedience to God, who is the source of life.

The depth and richness of meaning of the Lord's Supper are possible specifically because the Lord's Supper is a *symbolic* meal, yet we cannot speak of this as "just a symbol." What makes this an extraordinary meal is that it is a symbolic action of the people of God. Because it is a symbol, this meal occurs in space and time wherein the people of God are nourished by Christ. Therefore, we need to consider further the meaning of a symbol and particularly of a sacramental symbol.

2

THE SACRAMENTAL PRINCIPLE

Does It Make Any Difference?

Those who are skeptical about religious rites, particularly the sacramental actions of the Christian community, rightly wonder if these activities make a difference. Do they matter? Do they alter the equation of life and actually foster the values we so long to see take shape in our common life? Though much of what follows would apply equally to baptism, this study focuses on the Lord's Supper and asks, What difference, if any, does it make for the community of faith to participate in this holy meal?

The Lord's Supper is a rite that in some church traditions is practiced weekly and in others monthly and yet in others only a few times a year. Each tradition in which the meal is observed appreciates that this meal matters, and matters deeply. For some it is so important that they choose to observe it weekly. Others celebrate it only three or four times a year because of a conviction that it is so meaningful that it merits a special worship event and gathering. Either way, the Lord's Supper is a significant symbolic activity. Symbolic actions—religious and otherwise—make sense only if we understand what is happening, what the activity represents, and what it communicates. The holy meal of the church, then, merits time given to reflection as we reread the ancient text of Holy Scripture in a way that brings us into conversation with those who may see and read the text differently. The Lord's Supper, Holy Communion, the Eucharist—by whatever name—lies at the center of our worship and our common life. We need to make sense of it for ourselves, our children, and new Christians who join our communities of faith. We need to make sense of it so as to fellowship with Christians of other denominations and backgrounds. This celebration can be a source of worthwhile fellowship and unity rather than a cause of confusion, perplexity, or division.

Most of all, we need an understanding of this holy meal that enables us to meet and know Christ. In this meal, we encounter the ascended Lord Jesus, and the wonder of this meal is that through our eating and drinking, in the company of others, we are able to cultivate our union with Christ and our capacity to live in radical dependence on his grace and in genuine communion with other Christian believers.

The Meaning of a Symbol

Meaningful reflection on the Lord's Supper requires us to think *theologically* about this meal and then to consider our particular practices in light of Scripture and our theological heritage. The following considers the biblical texts that illuminate the meaning of this holy meal and also attends to how Christians of diverse backgrounds and traditions have understood this event in the life of the church. While this book has a twofold agenda—to read the biblical text afresh and to do so in a way that fosters mutual understanding and esteem among Christians—the approach taken is marked by a central concern that we recover an appreciation of *symbol* in our common life and, particularly, in our worship.

The Lord's Supper is *symbolic action*. Understanding this makes all the difference in our reading of Scripture and in our regard for how others view this meal. When Jesus said, "This is my body," he was using language in a way that is best engaged through an appreciation of symbol. I am always a little perplexed and intrigued when I hear someone refer to something as "just a symbol." I always wonder how anything can be a *mere* symbol.

By its very nature, a symbol is never just a symbol. We can say that a dog is just a dog or that a man is just a man, but a symbol is never just a symbol. It can, perhaps, be an empty symbol or a meaningless symbol, but it is never "just" a symbol. More often than not, a symbol or a symbolic action is alive with meaning, and its meaning and significance are deepened rather than diminished by frequent use. Further, its meaning can never be fully explained, for by its very nature, a symbol is multifaceted.

The mysterious and somewhat elusive character of symbols makes it vitally important that we appreciate their significance in our lives. By this I do not mean that we need to explain them. The very character of a symbol means that it cannot ever be fully explained. Rather, we need to attend to the significance of our symbols so that they have meaning for us and so that we participate in them in a manner that is congruent with our understanding. Symbols and symbolic actions merit our thoughtful consideration, especially when they matter to us as much, for example, as baptism and the Lord's Supper. Therefore, we do not in the end explain our use of symbolic actions, but theological consideration can and should deepen and enrich our practice of them.

Signs, Photographs, and Symbols

One of the most helpful ways to consider symbols is to contrast and compare them with signs and photographs. We use all three, and the similarities and differences are instructive.

Signs are important; it is difficult to imagine life without them. They help us navigate through the crossroads of our daily tasks and responsibilities. Life in a contemporary city would be impossible, for example, without traffic lights. Green means "go," we say. What we actually mean is that a green light indicates that one can proceed safely. Green does not mean "go" any more than red means "stop." There is no more "go-ness" in green than there is in red. The link between the sign and that which is signified is arbitrary. But in our social context, we have collectively agreed to allocate this particular meaning to a green light. Signs, then, point to something beyond themselves—a meaning that matters but a connection that is arbitrary. There is no inherent link or relationship between the sign and that which is signified. There is nothing intrinsic in the green light that gives it the meaning "go." But this is not the case with photographs.

While it is certainly possible to live without photographs, we can hardly conceive of life—family, relationships, and events in our world—without the photographs that capture significant moments and people. A portrait of a special person is a treasured possession; the photographs of special places are an important way by which we sustain vital memories. Photographs are different from signs. When I look at a photograph, the connection with what it represents or signifies is not arbitrary. The link is intrinsic, and it is this connection that makes the photograph meaningful. A photograph of my wife has so close an association with her that I will actually say, pointing at the picture, "This is my wife." Language allows us to make this kind of intimate association between the sign (in this case a photograph) and what is signified. It is this link that makes it meaningful.

Symbols are different from both signs and photographs. Appreciating how they are similar and how they are different provides helpful insight into the meaning of a sacramental action. Like signs, symbols point to another reality, but their meaning is more intangible and significant. They are not as clear and unambiguous as "green means go." Like photographs, symbols represent something, but in contrast to an image on paper, they do not necessarily resemble what they communicate.[1]

A symbol is an external, visible, and tangible object or action that represents an internal, intangible reality. A flag, for example, is a symbol of the hopes and aspirations of a people or a nation. In my culture, a ring on the fourth finger symbolizes a monogamous love commitment. A ritual can also be a symbol: Through a gesture, a movement, or a formal activity, we express something that is invisible but of vital significance.

---

1. Flags are used as symbols of national or cultural identities. The most powerful and meaningful flags are rarely those that are meant to look like anything. Sometimes countries try to represent as much as possible in their flags—as many values or elements of their country as they can picture. But the most evocative flags are usually the simplest. They do not try to "picture" the country or people but merely capture something central to their common identity.

A symbol is more like a sign than a photograph when we consider that it points to (rather than looks like) another reality. But a symbol is more like a photograph than a sign in that a photograph is much more evocative and engaging than a sign. When I enjoy a photograph of my wife, I am celebrating my wife; I am participating in the reality represented by the photograph. When I see a photograph of a place or an event, I am in a mysterious way engaging in that event, even if only distantly. What makes a symbol unique and special is that while it points to another reality, as does a sign, it also allows us to participate in that reality, much as with a photograph.

The key question, then, is one of meaning: To what do our symbols point? What do they signify? What is it that we engage in when we participate in our symbols? A wedding ring, the Olympic torch, a national flag all may be meaningless to those who do not assign significance to them or do not value what they symbolize. But when such symbols matter, they bespeak values, commitments, and passions. When I wear a wedding ring, I participate in what it represents—in what it means. When soccer fans wave the flag of their country during a game, it is a powerful declaration of their identity with the players on the field, who represent their country.

A symbol has even more significance when it comes to communal ritual activity. What makes a ritual a significant symbol is that we participate in it *together*. Together we identify with what is communicated through symbolic action. Whether we are blowing out candles on a birthday cake, standing by the side of the road awaiting the Olympic torch, throwing dirt on a casket, or waving a national flag, the power of the moment resides in the fact that we are not alone but are doing the act with others. These symbolic actions connect us with life, but more specifically, they connect us *to one another.* Ritual action enables us to be connected not only with the reality symbolized but also with one another.

Further, symbolic gestures and actions enable us to communicate realities far more deeply than is possible with words. We can speak together of the loss we experience with the death of a loved one, but nothing quite demonstrates this like the acts of walking together to the burial ground and watching as slowly and intentionally the body is lowered into the ground. Conversation cannot capture the force and meaning of these actions.

Sacraments

A sacrament is a symbol—something we can see, something we can touch, something we do together—that has religious or spiritual significance for a community of faith. A symbol is a sacrament not merely because it has a religious meaning or connotation. Rather, it is a sacrament because, first, it is ordained by Christ. While Christians of diverse traditions may differ as to how many sacraments Christ ordained, most if not all agree on the two central symbolic actions: baptism and the Lord's Supper. Second, what makes a symbol a sacrament is that it represents a spiritual reality that is held in common by those who participate in the action.

Thus, to participate in a sacrament is to participate in what is symbolized. Like a sign, a sacrament points to another reality without necessarily looking like that reality. A sacrament is an external symbol that is visual and sensory, but its primary significance is that it is a gesture, a communal act, or a ritual that points to and enables a community to join together in something of spiritual significance. What is noteworthy is the close connection between the symbol and what is symbolized, so close, indeed, that in human speech they are often identical, as with a photograph. I can hold up a picture of my grandchildren and say, "These are my grandsons," and no one wonders whether I am confused by a little piece of colored paper. We understand this kind of language; it is customary in our common life to use photographs and to speak of symbols in this way. To take this kind of language literally would miss the point and would rob us of both the capacity to use language well and the wonderful gift of symbols. Without symbols, our lives would be flat and one-dimensional. Symbols and sacraments enrich our lives, enabling us to engage spiritual reality with heart and mind, indeed, with our whole selves.

Jesus said, "This is my body," even though what he had in his hands was clearly not his body. He was using the language of symbol. The bread is like a sign in that it points to another reality.

The symbol does not *look* like his body. But it is also like a photograph in that when we participate in the Lord's Supper, we enter into what is symbolized. The relationship between the symbol and the reality is so immediate that Jesus can say, "This is my body." The connection between the two is so close, so intimate that if we discount the symbol we discount what is symbolized. If we neglect the symbol, we neglect what is symbolized. Jesus ordains—commands—his disciples to eat and drink. Yes, it is an invitation to a meal, but it is also a command. For his followers, life depends on it; their relationship with Jesus depends on it. Sacraments are never *just* symbols. They are the very means by which we participate in the intangible and spiritual realities without which there is no life.

Some Christians insist that a sacrament cannot be a means of grace. They suggest that to think this way is like saying that when you come to a stop sign on the highway, the stop sign will somehow stop your car. They insist that in such situations you must apply the brake; *you* must stop the car. There is no inherent "stopness" in the sign. Without the personal action of stopping the car, the sign is useless. But this kind of thinking about sacraments fails to appreciate that sacraments are symbols. The difference is, while a stop sign indicates appropriate action, a sacrament actually communicates what is symbolized.

Some contemporary studies on symbol and ritual are helpful in reflecting on the character of sacramental actions. Ronald L. Grimes, in his book *Deeply into the Bone: Re-inventing Rites of Passage*,[2] stresses that ritual is of extraordinary value to human life because it is an activity in which value and meaning are no longer merely cerebral but, in his words, lodge in the bone, in its very marrow. He suggests that technology is increasingly breeding "technological values" in our bones. He notes that in North America, birth is now largely a biomedical event. Grimes goes on to suggest that we urgently need to reformulate and embrace rites of passage that are human and empowering—rites of passage that enable a person to come into the world in a way that is familial. For an individual to come of age with strong familial and community bonds, there needs to be a communal rite of

2. Ronald L. Grimes, *Deeply into the Bone: Re-inventing Rites of Passage*, Life Passage Series (Berkeley: University of California Press, 2000).

passage for this person. The marriage rite prepares newlyweds to live within the social complexities they will inevitably face and binds them not only to one another but to the community that participates with them in the marriage celebration. Grimes makes related comments on the rites of passage associated with death.

What Grimes says has special significance for the Christian church, particularly for those Christians who are ambivalent about symbols and rituals. Every generation has had Christians who question the validity of the sacraments—the symbolic actions of the church. They have concluded that these are empty symbols, meaningless because they are nothing more than a performance. They discount the external symbolic action out of a conviction that what really matters is the internal experience. Yet the irony is that ritual activity—sacramental actions—have the potential to cultivate within people the very values for which they long. Grimes's observations call us to a recognition that if our values, convictions, and faith are going to be "bred in the bone," we need to appreciate the power and the significance of ritual as the embodied way in which this happens. Further, a common symbolic act—or sacrament—keeps our spirituality from being just internal and individual. Sacramental actions keep spirituality truly communal. By these acts, our common faith and our common experience of Christ are "bred in our bones." Thus, the Lord's Supper is the act of the Christian community, of the church as the church.

A Theological Perspective

Jesus said, "This is my body." Appreciating what he meant by this brings together a confluence of three theological principles. Each is a lens by which to view this event in the life of the Christian community.

The first lens is the *creation* principle. The Christian theological tradition affirms the inherent goodness of creation. Clearly, the world and all God's creatures are infected by sin. We live in a fragmented world; creation has gone askew. Nevertheless, the biblical perspective on matter, on the physical, affirms that creation itself is good. More to the point, creation is a vehicle by which God is known. The created order is a medium of divine revelation. Christians insist that it is a major philosophical mistake to assume that only that which is visible exists. The materialist fails to "see" anything beyond the immediate and the tangible and thus concludes that there is no spirit, no God, and nothing beyond the concrete. But the opposite error is also a philosophical misstep—the vision of reality that assumes that matter does not count, that it has no meaning and no inherent relationship with God and the transcendent. In contrast, a biblical perspective on matter affirms the inherent value and goodness of the physical, the tangible, the concrete. The sacramental principle recognizes that all of creation is a potential vehicle for the knowledge and grace of God.

The second theological principle that serves as a lens for understanding symbol and sacrament is the *incarnation*. The incarnation affirms the extraordinary reality that God took on human flesh in the person of the Lord Jesus Christ. The incarnation is a central tenet of the Christian faith and echoes and affirms the creation principle. As with creation, our belief in the incarnation leads us to appreciate the physical and the tangible: The Son of God took on flesh (John 1:14). God is known and graces the world through the incarnate One. Christ, in this sense, is the sacrament of God. The glory of the incarnation is that the physicality of Jesus—his human nature—is the very means by which God is known. In other words, the humanity of Jesus was not an obstacle to God's revelation that we somehow need to look past to find God. On the contrary, the humanity of Jesus, his tangible, physical, material presence, was and is the way by which God is known through Jesus. The incarnation is the ultimate declaration of what is proclaimed repeatedly in Genesis 1: God saw what he had made, and it was good.

A third lens through which we view the Christian perspective on symbol and sacrament is the theological principle of the *church*. The church is the body of Christ in the world. The people of God—the community of faith—are the life and presence of Christ in the world. The church is not one and the same as the Lord Jesus Christ. Rather, the church is the sacrament of Christ; it is the presence of the risen and living Christ in the world. In this capacity, the church shows forth the grace of Christ and the glory of the gospel in both word and deed—by what we proclaim and what we do. In our speaking and our acting, we reveal Christ and make him known.

The sacramental actions of the church—baptism and the Lord's Supper—are concrete, tangible, and visible means by which the church takes the very stuff of creation, water, bread, and cup, and in response to the invitation and command of Christ reenacts the wonder of the gospel. In so doing, the material creation is a means by which God's grace is known.

The Approach Taken in This Book

All of this makes sense only when we have a grasp of the meaning of the Lord's Supper. This is the central symbolic action of the church ordained by Christ and celebrated week after week. But what does it mean? Probing the meaning does not drain it of its power and significance. On the contrary, by a theological exploration of this act, we sustain its vital role in our lives. A. W. Tozer has aptly defined a sacrament as "an external expression of an inward grace."[3] We then rightly ask, What is the grace that is symbolized through this external expression, the Lord's Supper?

As mentioned, the approach taken in this study of the Lord's Supper is twofold. First, it is an invitation to read or reread the familiar biblical texts. The following chapters consider one or more of these texts through an exposition of a word. I have identified seven words that illumine the meaning of the Lord's Supper.

Second, this book seeks to highlight the diversity of perspective that the church brings to its understanding of the Lord's Supper. There has been considerable debate about the Lord's Supper. The church's history is rife with anathemas delivered by one Christian denomination against another, discounting, if

3. A. W. Tozer, *The Pursuit of God* (Harrisburg, PA: Christian Publications, 1948), 121. By implication, then, Tozer insists that we can celebrate the human body and our embodiment. In other words, a high view of the sacraments goes with a positive view of the body (and vice versa). A clear and biblical theology of the incarnation gives us yet another perspective on the interplay between the interior experience and the sacramental action.

not actually condemning, the other's conception and practice of this holy meal.

But we are now in a period of the church's history alive with possibilities of renewed understanding and engagement. Christians are learning from one another and appreciating one another to a degree rarely experienced (if ever) in the history of the Christian faith. This study of the Lord's Supper is, hopefully, an example of just such an endeavor. I will profile various views on the Lord's Supper and demonstrate how we can learn from one another and appreciate the diversity that we bring to the meaning of this holy meal. What we learn from others enhances rather than diminishes our appreciation of this sacrament. If we are open to learning from others, we can discover different perspectives that will enrich our own participation in the Lord's Supper.

Part of the reason we need to listen to others is that different traditions have often focused on, or at least given more attention to, some biblical texts over against others. By listening to others we are drawn to texts on the Lord's Supper that we might otherwise miss or pass by in our own reading. Thus, while I indicated that the approach taken in this book is twofold—a rereading of biblical texts and a consideration of diverse theological perspectives—in fact, the two dovetail. A *biblical* reading is an *ecumenical* reading. Our reading of Scripture is enriched when we consider how other Christians read the Bible and practice the Lord's Supper. Scripture is and must be the final authority and guide to an understanding of the Lord's Supper. However, the Spirit has allowed diverse theological and spiritual traditions to profile different views concerning the Lord's Supper, so much so that we can only truly read the biblical text if we learn to listen to one another.

However, there is a caution. One of the temptations in learning from other traditions is to discount one's own. Actually, the reverse should happen. As we encounter and learn from others, we should cultivate an appreciation of our own Christian heritage, our own upbringing. A meditation on the meaning of the Lord's Supper enables us to dig deeper and with gratitude renew the practices and the understanding of the Lord's Supper within our own Christian community. In other words, what we seek as we learn from one another is a deeper appreciation of the richness of this holy meal. In this process, we may choose to reconsider some of our practices, but that is a by-product of our study. The central objective is that we come to a renewed appreciation of our own tradition and practices, an appreciation informed by other traditions and, most of all, by a renewed reading of the biblical text.[4]

The Cross and the Resurrection

An affirmation of diversity of perspective on the Lord's Supper is not a declaration that anything goes or that all views on the meaning of the Lord's Supper or all practices are equally valid. Instead, a critical reflection on the theological significance of the Lord's Supper should enhance our capacity to be discerning Christians, to make judgments about both meaning and practice.[5] The call to discernment brings to mind three considerations:

1. the proclamation of Christ Jesus risen and crucified
2. the presence of the Spirit and the body of Christ
3. the need to have a theologically informed practice of the Lord's Supper

What makes the celebration of the holy meal a *Christian* celebration is that the Lord's Supper is ultimately about Jesus Christ—incarnate, crucified, risen, ascended, sender of the Spirit, and triumphant King. At the heart of the gospel is the dual act of the cross and the resurrection. The chapters that follow explore each of the different dimensions of meaning, and I hope to demonstrate the marvel of how a single meal can represent

4. I should acknowledge that in this study I will not hesitate to give my opinions. But what I want to stress is that I do so not so much to say that "I am right" as to stir up our thinking and conversation.

5. Grimes also notes that "if rites drive meaning to the marrow, then the criticism of rites must cut to the bone" (*Deeply into the Bone*, 7). The danger is that rites of passage could be not only ineffectual but also downright oppressive. It is a stinging reminder that it is possible to have either senseless or vacuous rituals or rituals that unwittingly communicate in ways that are contrary to the fundamental meaning of the gospel.

so much. But the wealth and the diversity of meaning should never distract us from the central reality of this meal: In eating and drinking together, we are encountering the crucified and risen Christ.

Further, we also need to ask, If Christ is present in this event, *how* is Christ present? The answer will inevitably bring us to a consideration of the ministry of the Holy Spirit in our common life. If, as the Nicene Creed puts it so eloquently, the Spirit is "the Lord and Giver of Life," how does this find expression in the Lord's Supper? What is the relationship between the Spirit and the sacrament?

Finally, as we explore the meaning of the Lord's Supper, it should become apparent that our practices mean something. They have theological content. We do what we do for a reason, and what we do should reflect a range of theological convictions. What are we doing? And why do we do it?

When it comes to practice, one of the important reminders is that part of the genius of a symbol is its simplicity. There is little if any need for variety or novelty. Indeed, the power and effectiveness of symbolic action come from the fact that we do it again and again in the very same way. Therefore, this book will not propose new and novel ways to celebrate the Lord's Supper, as though innovation and variety would help make celebration of the Lord's Supper more meaningful. The opposite is the case. We will see how important it is, if the grace of God is going to premeate all of life deeply and thoroughly, to have consistency rather than variety, continuity rather than novelty, and routine rather than change.

PART 2

SEVEN WORDS

3

REMEMBRANCE

The Lord's Supper as a Memorial

And when he had given thanks, he broke it and said, "This is my body that is for you. Do this in remembrance of me." In the same way he took the cup also, after supper, saying, "This cup is the new covenant in my blood. Do this, as often as you drink it, in remembrance of me." For as often as you eat this bread and drink the cup, you proclaim the Lord's death until he comes.

1 Corinthians 11:24–26

As a young person I was regularly reminded in church that the Lord's Supper is a memorial meal, no more and no less. Typical of many evangelical congregations, we celebrated the Lord's Supper once a month. On the first Sunday of each month, the elements were stacked high in aluminum containers on the communion table, which was covered with a white tablecloth. The elements were bits of cracker along with thumb-sized cups of grape juice. This all took place at the end of the worship service, and as a result, worship on the first Sunday of the month always lasted a little longer. It was invariably a solemn time of reflection, meditation, and, of course, "remembrance."

On the other Sundays of the month, the table was left un-covered, though sometimes it held a bouquet of flowers. But the words of the Lord's Supper remained, carved into the oak on the front of the table: "Do this in remembrance of me." We had no doubt about the meaning of the Lord's Supper: It is a memorial.

While I hope to stress that the Lord's Supper is much more than a memorial, it is indeed a memorial, and this is an ap-propriate place to begin our reflections on the meaning of this sacred event. We gather and celebrate by eating and drinking together in remembrance of Christ. But this event in the life of the Christian community calls for a particular and unique kind of remembering.

First, it is important to stress that this act of remembrance is not sentimental nostalgia. For some, acts of remembering are little more than futile attempts to live in the past. Some people are more attuned to the past they hold in their minds than to their present experience and reality. They look back nostalgically on a past event that for them can never be matched by the present. Special memories are celebrated in a way that diminishes their capacity to enjoy and relish the present moment. We find this kind of "memory" in our places of work and in the church com-munities of which we are a part. People hark back to a previous time that, inevitably, is a better time, and they wish that things could be as they used to be.

Part of the problem with this perspective is that past events are just that: They are past. We can try to hold on, somehow, to ma-terial things, language, ideas, and feelings as a matter of personal interest in "history." But the danger is that when people relive a golden age of the past—from their own personal history or the history of a people or a church or an organization, a period that may strike them as more interesting or less complicated than their own age—they are not truly connected to the present. You may hear some Christians speak of that old-time religion, which for them brings to mind associations linked with an earlier time in their lives. Some people love to relive a military battle of the past. They do not visit a battle scene to ask what it might mean for us today and to appreciate its symbolic significance. Rather, they enact the battle itself, with all the noise, smoke, dust, and old uniforms in an attempt to relive a scene of glory and heroism. Their love of the past both idealizes that past and also keeps them from truly living in the present.

Such remembering does not serve people well. We may remember the details or the specifics of what happened in the past, but memories serve us well only if they enable us to be fully present in the here and now and grant us courage to face tomorrow. Nostalgic sentimentalism is not true remembering. An authentic act of remembrance allows the past to inform and animate the present; it enables us to be fully present for current challenges and opportunities, to relish what we have now and to face the future with hope.

Second, the act of remembrance, in a spiritual sense, is not one of remembering *everything*. Yes, we must live in light of the past. Yes, we need to learn how to remember well so that we can live well. Without a doubt we learn from the past. Our personal histories are a vital source of encouragement and wisdom. But a constructive remembering, one that animates the present and sustains us for the future, is necessarily *selective*.

In *The Last Gift of Time: Life beyond Sixty*,[1] a book on aging, Carolyn G. Heilbrun suggests that one of the curses on the old is that they remember far too much. Heilbrun suggests that to age graciously is to let some things go, particularly the ways we have been wronged, criticized, overlooked, and wounded. We must learn to dis-remember, to let some things go from our remembering, for there is nothing to be gained, nothing to be learned from some memories. We must choose actually to bury some memories under the sands of time.

I can recall meeting people who can with vivid description recall a wrong that was done to them. They rehearse it again and again; reliving it in their imagination almost seems to make it more grievous with each retelling. They are, essentially, living in the past, in this case, in the wrongs of the past.

Yet at the same time, there is a need to recall events such as the holocaust, where a loss of memory means a denial of history. Elie Wiesel, the American Jewish writer, has rightly stressed the need to sustain a memory "lest we forget." Such a forgetting

---

1. Carolyn G. Heilbrun, *The Last Gift of Time: Life beyond Sixty* (New York: Ballantine Books, 1997), 115–17.

would be an irresponsible oversight of an event that in effect suggests it did not happen. To forget is to deny.

Thus, from Wiesel and others we come to an appreciation that in the Judeo-Christian spiritual tradition, remembrance is intentional and deeply spiritual: We choose to remember. In so doing, we are enabled to live in truth, assuring that our present is not disconnected from but deeply informed by the past. And then, also, we remember in order to give thanks. But the remembering is selective; we choose what from the past is worth remembering and must be remembered to enable us to live in faith, hope, and love. The past is not a golden age to be rehearsed with nostalgia. Rather, it is a retelling of those events of the past that matters. The telling of the past instructs, informs, and encourages us to live in the present in light of the past—particularly those events in the past that we believe must shape the contours of our present.

For some, the present is everything. There is no history; there is nothing to remember because the past is irrelevant. From this perspective, life is only the passing of seasons. No one event is more significant than another; each season erases the previous season. Nothing in the past matters.

The biblical perspective, however, allows the past to shape, inform, and transform our present and give significance to our lives, our relationships, and our work. I am a married man. The fact of my wedding matters profoundly in describing who I am. It is an event that determines, demarcates, and gives meaning to my life. I only live truthfully, and thus in freedom, when I live in light of this event—when my present is informed and defined by this past event.

As Christians, nothing so marks our lives as the death and resurrection of Christ Jesus. Thus, there is extraordinary import to the words Jesus said to his disciples immediately prior to his death: "Do this in remembrance of me" (1 Cor. 11:24). He ate with them, and he affirmed that this holy meal would be a *memorial.* Each time they ate this meal, they would remember him and his work.

The church has been well served by recent theological reflection on the Greek word that Jesus uses here, the term *anamnesis,* "to remember." Much more than just the idea of recalling, *anamnesis* reflects the Hebrew use of the word *zkr,* which is usually translated "remember" and specifically implies that we live in

38

the present and behave in the present in light of our memory. It is memory that gives meaning to our present. In this sense, in the Lord's Supper we remember those events that, more than any others, shape the course of human history and identify who we are as followers of Christ. This act of remembrance is one in which the past shapes, informs, and penetrates the present. We live now, in our work, in our relationships, indeed, in each dimension of our lives, as a people for whom everything is altered, for good, by the reality of Christ Jesus' death and resurrection.

But there is more. In our act of remembrance, we discover and affirm that we are not merely looking back; in the memorial meal, the crucified and risen Christ himself is present. This is crucial. It is not our work of remembrance that carries the day. The communion service is not merely a cerebral, intellectual activity wherein, as best we can, we look back and recall what Christ has done for us and then, again as best we can, we consider what it means for us to live in light of the cross and resolve that we will live in such a manner.

All too frequently, this is what seems to happen in a communion service. It becomes an event of *thinking*—of recalling the death of Christ and then of resolving to live a life appropriate to what has been recalled. The problem with this is that the communion service becomes our work, and the "benefits" depend on how much appropriate thinking we can do matched by the strength of our resolve.

A communion service is not merely about recalling the good news of the death and resurrection of Christ. In our remembering, the risen Christ himself is present. Communion, then, is not the same as a memorial service to remember and honor someone who has died. This holy meal is a memorial of a different kind. It is a recollection and a remembrance that take us into an encounter with the very one whom we remember. The most significant thing that happens, then, is not that we do this work of remembrance. Rather, in our remembering, we are entering into the most vital and life-giving events of all: the death and resurrection of Christ Jesus. In our remembering, the crucified and risen Christ is in our midst. As we will see in the chapters that are to come, this means that Christ is our host at this meal. He is present, and by his Spirit he enables us to live in the grace of God.

Since Christ is the host of the meal, and very much present in the celebration of the Lord's Supper, the focus and central dynamic of the event are in the present, not the past. We are not, then, reliving or reenacting a past event—neither the event of the cross nor the event of the Last Supper. We are, rather, allowing a past event to shape and inform the present.

The Dual Proclamation

In the memorial of the Lord's Supper, Christ is present. But more, the death of Christ is declared. There is a close affinity between the act of remembrance and the act of proclamation. In the words of institution in 1 Corinthians, Paul recalls the words of Jesus, "Do this in remembrance of me," and then adds, "For as often as you eat this bread and drink this cup, you proclaim the Lord's death until he comes" (11:26). What this means is that in our worship there is a *dual* proclamation. First, we have the Word. The gospel is preached through the exposition of Scripture. Second, there is also symbolic, ritual action. Two kinds of proclamation take place, one in *word* and the other in *deed*—in what we say and then in what we do. The one is a verbal symbol. The other is a visible and gestural symbol. But both proclaim. Both are a declaration and a manifestation of the gospel.

We speak not merely with words; we speak and communicate through nonverbal ritual actions and symbols. In a sense, the ring on my finger proclaims my commitment to one woman. A candle, lit while we worship, proclaims our conviction that the risen Christ is present in our worship. It is important to emphasize that symbols by themselves mean little. It is simply a lit candle unless we agree and declare together the meaning of the symbol. The ring on my finger is just a piece of metal unless words accompany the symbol. Christ has ordained the symbolic action of the holy meal, but it has meaning only when it accompanies the Word—proclaimed, preached, declared.

Conversely, worship is one-dimensional and cerebral if we engage the gospel only through the verbal proclamation in Word and view the sacramental action as secondary or supplemental. Our redemption is in word and deed. Jesus comes to us not only as a teacher but also as the incarnate One who acts on our behalf. In the *act* of the cross, not only in the words he speaks, he proclaims his love for the world and for each of us. However, while the cross is absolutely essential—the deed that accompanies the words—this event or act alone makes no sense unless Jesus proclaims the coming of the kingdom and through his apostles declares, verbally, the gospel. Both are needed. The one makes sense only in light of the other. The one authenticates and enhances the other.

Both word and deed enable us to know and experience union with Christ. However, they *are* different. It is important to stress that they are different, for the difference helps us appreciate the meaning and place of the sacramental action. If no distinction is made, the Lord's Supper is redundant.

An appreciation of the difference between the two recalls a historic emphasis in Reformed theology, the primacy of the ministry of the Word. The basis for this perspective is the conviction that the Word can *be* without the sacraments but that the sacraments cannot *be* without the Word. The Word can stand on its own. It makes sense on its own. The sacramental actions, however, have meaning and significance only in tandem with the Word. Thus, the sacraments are secondary, not in the sense that they are of less significance or importance but that they are dependent on the witness of the Word. To put it differently, the actions in the sacraments become symbols—and thus sacramental events—only when they are accompanied by the Word.

However, this is the case with all things, not just sacraments. Everything is dependent on the Word; the whole testimony of Scripture reminds us that we live by the Word of God.[2] This is echoed in the call to both Timothy and Titus in the Pastoral Epistles. We note there an unequivocal emphasis on the priority of the ministry of the Word. The sacramental action, then, is seen as "added" to the Word or as "following" the Word. It is appropriate that in the order of worship—the liturgy of the church—the Lord's Supper always follows the Word. It is the Word that gives the Lord's Supper its meaning.

However, G. C. Berkouwer, the Dutch Reformed theologian, stresses that although we affirm the primacy of the Word, the

---

2. See, for example, the words of the prophet in Isaiah 55, where he calls his readers to yearn for the life-giving Word of God.

sacraments are not secondary in any sense that would discount or degrade them.[3] He notes that the Reformers, especially Calvin, Luther, and the Anglican Reformers, placed a high value on the sacramental actions of the church—much higher than much of contemporary evangelicalism, which claims to be an heir to the Reformation. Further, the Reformers never set Word and sacrament over against each other. Both were consistently viewed as a means of grace.

The sacrament of the Lord's Supper gives us something we would not otherwise experience and which we need in order to know the full measure of God's grace. Through the holy meal we know and experience Christ in a way that we would not otherwise know and experience him. Just as baptism necessarily accompanies the Word that calls us to faith, the action of the Lord's Supper necessarily accompanies the preached Word that sustains our faith. It is necessary *because* it is different and complementary; it is a different form of proclamation. What makes it different is precisely that it is a symbol—a ritual action within the community of faith.

The Power of Ritual Action

The holy table does not simply serve as a symbolic proclamation—a proclamation in action. It is also a proclamation *through* this very action. We declare the gospel through gesture, through the act of eating and drinking. It is this ritual action of eating and drinking that makes this event truly an act of remembrance. Through the action of eating and drinking, our remembrance is not merely cerebral but an act of our whole being. We remember through the most fundamental of actions—eating and drinking.

We need to come to the table regularly, when we feel like it and when we don't, for the great danger is that we would forget. We can so easily forget. I do not mean that we no longer recall or believe that something happened. Rather, our forgetting is one of no longer living aligned with the reality and wonder of

---

3. G. C. Berkouwer, *The Sacraments* (Grand Rapids: Eerdmans, 1969), 43.

Christ's death and resurrection. We fail to live in the light of this ancient event. So easily through neglect the cross and the resurrection no longer penetrate our present, enabling us to live in the light of the gospel.

We can understand why this can happen. Our lives are inundated with details, problems, challenges, temptations, and distractions. And when all is well, we are easily distracted by our comfort and ease! When we are bored, we are easily overcome by our own boredom.

And so we must eat and drink. We must act out our remembrance, and we need to do it often in the company of the people of God. When we do, through the grace of Christ, our lives are anchored in history. Our faith is not merely mental, something we hold in our minds as best we can as we seek to concentrate and not forget what we should remember. Rather, through the symbolic action we do more than merely recall; we remember. We eat in remembrance specifically that we might remember. But more, this act calls us to give thanks, as those who remember, and then actually *enables* us to live the whole of life with thanksgiving, our lives infused with the gospel. Then we not only see and hear the truth but are also enabled to *live* the truth. As regular, routine action, along with the proclamation of the Word, this holy meal gives clarity, meaning, and purpose to our lives.

4

COMMUNION

The Lord's Supper as Fellowship with Christ and with One Another

Therefore, my dear friends, flee from the worship of idols. I speak as to sensible people; judge for yourselves what I say. The cup of blessing that we bless, is it not a sharing in the blood of Christ? The bread that we break, is it not a sharing in the body of Christ? Because there is one bread, we who are many are one body, for we all partake of the one bread. . . .

Whoever, therefore, eats the bread or drinks the cup of the Lord in an unworthy manner will be answerable for the body and blood of the Lord. Examine yourselves, and only then eat of the bread and drink of the cup. For all who eat and drink without discerning the body, eat and drink judgment against themselves. For this reason many of you are weak and ill, and some have died. But if we judged ourselves, we would not be judged. But when we are judged by the Lord, we are disciplined so that we may not be condemned along with the world. So then, my brothers and sisters, when you come together to eat, wait for one another. If you are hungry, eat at home, so that when you come together, it will not be for your condemnation. About the other things I will give instructions when I come.

1 Corinthians 10:14–17; 11:27–34

The human person is not designed to be alone; we are not wired to live in isolation from one another as spiritual monads or hermits. To be fully human, to live in the joy of all that we are called to be, requires that we are in fellowship with God and with others. This communion with God and others is fundamental to life.

This does not discount both the legitimacy of and the need for solitude. In solitude we are in fellowship with the Creator, and a connection with God is the necessary precursor to true communion with our fellow human beings. The Christian spiritual tradition affirms the integrity of each human person as distinct, and each human person has the potential for an intimate relationship with the Creator. This is reflected in the spiritual practice of solitude. But the tragedy of the fall is that solitude becomes an autonomous act. We were created to hunger after God and for fellowship with the Creator; this intimacy is made possible through radical dependence. Out of this dependence on God we are called into community with one another—a fellowship that, in turn, sustains our fellowship with God. The affirmation of community and the need for fellowship with God, therefore, are not denials of the individual person and the need for solitude. We must not confuse community with a communalism that destroys or compromises the distinctive identity of each person. True solitude is necessarily complemented by community.

Thus, the first and greatest command that Jesus gave in his proclamation of the gospel is to love God and to love our neighbor as ourselves. We turn from autonomy and enter into fellowship with God and one another. Both dimensions of communion—relationship with God and relationship with others—are mediated, made possible, and sustained by Christ Jesus. God is known through Christ, and our relationship with one another, authentic and life-giving fellowship, is made possible and is sustained by Christ. We cannot live in communion with one another except through the gracious presence of Christ.

Nowhere is this more powerfully expressed than in the Lord's Supper. This event is one in which we declare that life is found in communion with God and with one another. But more, in this event, communion with God and others is actually sustained. Thus, it is fitting, as we find particularly in Anglican-Episcopalian

46

circles, to call the sacred meal Holy Communion. In 1 Corinthians 10, the apostle speaks of a communion—*koinonia*—with the body and blood of Christ Jesus. This word could also be translated "participation" or "fellowship." What is noteworthy is that two events are sustained and renewed simultaneously: the relationship of the community with Christ, of God's people with their Lord, and second, the relationship of human persons with one another. Though the Roman Catholic tradition has tended to emphasize sacrifice and to downplay the reality that the Lord's Supper is an event of communion, the great Catholic theologian Thomas Aquinas wrote, "There are two realities signified by the sacrament: one is contained in the sacrament, namely Christ himself, and the other signified but not contained, namely the mystical body of Christ, the companionship of the saints."[1]

In the Lord's Supper, we are not merely eating; we are eating *together*. There is a companionship with Christ, surely, but it is a communal event. We are in fellowship with Christ, and we are in fellowship with one another. Table fellowship, while declaring that we are in fellowship with Christ and one another, also cultivates and enables this fellowship. When we eat together as families and friends, we simultaneously affirm our shared identity and cultivate our unity.

The Lord's Supper is an act of Holy Communion—with Christ and with one another. Both are equally significant dimensions of what it means to participate in this sacred meal. On the one hand, our fellowship is derivative of our communion with Christ, and, on the other, we know this communion with Christ only when we are in fellowship with one another. Our experience of Christ is mediated to us through the community of faith. Nevertheless, our relationship with Christ is primary. It may not be experientially primary; it could well be that our experience of Christ follows our experience of the community of faith. But the community is always derived from Christ, who is its head and life source.

This is worth noting because it is so easy for the Christian community to become nothing more than a religious society or club and not a fellowship whose life is derivative of the life of Christ.

1. Thomas Aquinas, *Summa Theologiae: A Concise Translation*, ed. Timothy McDermott (Westminster, MD: Christian Classics, 1989), 587 (80/1).

In much contemporary worship, the Lord's Supper has become little more than an affirmation of our human fellowship. It has become a solemn, ritual endorsement of a relationship we have with one another and our warm feelings toward one another. All of this has its place, but the basis for our fellowship is always the fact that together, in this event, we proclaim the Lord's death. We are gathered in the company of Christ. Our fellowship is given meaning by the death and resurrection of Christ Jesus, and it is the living Christ who calls us together and enables us to be in communion with one another. Our practice of the Lord's Supper should always make it abundantly clear that our host is the Lord and that this is first of all an encounter with him. If this is not evident, we can easily fall into a sentimentalized version of Christian community in which what binds us together is not our common faith but other values and criteria.[2]

Fellowship with Christ

Richard Baxter, the great Puritan, boldly suggested that "no where is God so near to man as in Jesus Christ; and no where is Christ so familiarly represented to us, as in his holy sacrament."[3] No single act of the community of faith so thoroughly brings us into and sustains our fellowship with Christ as the holy meal.

2. Thus, Dietrich Bonhoeffer observes that Christian community is a spiritual not a psychic reality precisely because it "is founded solely on Jesus Christ," or as he puts it earlier in that same work, "The ground and strength and promise of all our community is in Jesus Christ alone" (Dietrich Bonhoeffer, *Works*, vol. 5, *Life Together: Prayerbook of the Bible*, trans. Daniel W. Bloesch, ed. Geffrey B. Kelly [Minneapolis: Fortress, 1996], 38). One of the great strengths of the Anabaptist, Baptist, and Mennonite traditions is the emphasis in the Lord's Supper on the gathered community. For these traditions, the elements are secondary and certainly not in themselves the "presence" of Christ. The "real presence" is found not in the elements but in the community of faith, the body of Christ *gathered*. As will be stressed below, this emphasis on the gathered community is an essential and necessary perspective; we are doing this *together*. But we also need to emphasize that this is not merely the gathering of the community. It is the community gathered in the presence of its living Head, and something—the elements perhaps—needs to signal this.

3. Quoted in J. I. Packer, *A Quest for Godliness: The Puritan Vision of the Christian Life* (Wheaton: Crossway, 1990), 213.

When Paul speaks of the Lord's Supper as a participation in the blood and body of Christ, he is, in part, stressing that table fellowship is a significant and intimate spiritual event. He is speaking to the matter of meals held in conjunction with temple worship. His readers seem naïve about the meaning of these meals; they do not comprehend that their participation violates their Christian identity because such meals are acts of encounter and communion with the gods. In the ancient world, to eat with another was considered a spiritual act—a declaration of and a participation in a spiritual relationship. This has direct application for the Christian community. In the Lord's Supper, we are in communion—not merely declaring but actually entering into a fellowship—with the ascended Lord Jesus Christ. It is an immediate encounter with the risen Christ. Jesus is the host of the meal. In the Lord's Supper, we experience both his welcome to the meal and his "peace be with you" as we return to the world. This event is an actual encounter. Christ is present, Christ is host, Christ welcomes and blesses. We are in actual—not virtual—fellowship with Jesus.

Fellowship with One Another

The complement to our fellowship with Christ is our fellowship with one another. The Lord's Supper is a rite of reconciliation: Our peace is with Christ and with one another. When we meet, we discern both the presence of the risen Christ, who hosts the meal, and also the body, the community of faith of which we are a part.

The Lord's Supper, then, is never a solitary and individual event. It is always a meal of the community of faith hosted by Christ as an event wherein we both declare and experience the grace that we are at peace with one another (Col. 3:15). The unity of the community of faith is always vulnerable and tenuous, and the common act of eating together sustains and nurtures this unity. Thus, we can legitimately come to this table only if we are at peace with one another. We come without grievance or complaint, or, as we read in 1 Timothy 2:8, we come without quarreling. We do not come with malice against our sisters and brothers (Col. 3:13). Indeed, as Thomas Aquinas puts it, the Eucharist is "the sacramental sign of church unity."[4] It is the declaration—by ritual sign—that we are at peace with one another.

We declare this peace when we greet one another and welcome one another to both the event of worship and the meal itself. In the language of Romans 15:7, we welcome one another as Christ welcomed us. We grant one another the "holy kiss"—the declaration that we are at peace. We receive the other, we forgive the other, we bear the sins of the other. There is no other way to come to this table. If we are not at peace with one another, we commit a travesty, an affront before the holy table.

In many churches, at some point in the service those present are urged to greet those around them. But a friendly hello usually pales in comparison with the ancient act of exchanging a holy greeting or kiss, known in more liturgical circles as the "passing of the peace." Rightly understood, this is an act by which one declares, in greeting those in one's immediate vicinity, that there is peace—forgiveness and acceptance—between them. People declare with confidence, in the name of Christ, "The peace of Christ be with you" and hear the classic response, "And also with you!"

This is an ancient practice. Early in the history of the church, believers recognized that a formal act of this nature was a worthwhile way of expressing the assurance that they participated in the holy meal as people who were in communion with Christ and one another. The early church father Cyril of Jerusalem, speaking of the call to receive and greet one another with a holy kiss, put it this way:

> You must not suppose that this is the usual kind of kiss which ordinary friends exchange when they meet in the street. This kiss is different. By it souls are united with one another and receive a pledge of the mutual forgiveness of all wrong. So then, a kiss is a sign of the union of souls and of the expulsion of all remembrance of wrong. . . . So the kiss means reconciliation, and is therefore holy.[5]

The elements themselves are also a means by which we declare that we are at peace with one another. The loaf of bread—single

---

4. Aquinas, *Summa Theologiae*, 568 (73/1).

5. Cyril of Jerusalem, "On the Mysteries 4 and 5," in *Documents in Early Christian Thought*, ed. Maurice Wiles and Mark Santer (Cambridge: Cambridge University Press, 1975), 190–92.

and whole—declares that we are one (1 Cor. 10:17).[6] The table symbolizes our mutual acceptance and also our commitment to love and serve one another. The Lord's Supper, then, is more than just a celebration of human goodwill and comradery; it is both an act of acceptance and a commitment to generous service.

It is important to indicate, however, that such peace does not necessarily mean that we come to the meal with no strained or difficult relationships, even potentially severed relationships. Here is where the language of Romans 12:18 is helpful. Paul urges his readers to be at peace with everyone, insofar as it is possible and as far as it depends on them. In other words, we are responsible to do all we can to be at peace with others before we come to the table. We may come knowing that even though a relationship is not healed—not yet, at least—we have done all we can.

In such cases, we cannot despair for the relationship or for our capacity in general to live in peace with others, for the Lord's Supper declares our peace and our resolve to live in fellowship with one another and is also the central means by which this unity and peace are enabled and fostered.

So we come to the table with hope, even for strained and difficult relationships. We receive the grace that enables us to accept others, forgive others, love others, and, as God enables, live in peace with others insofar as it depends on us.

Discerning the Body

It is necessary in this regard to comment on the sobering words of the apostle Paul found in 1 Corinthians 11 and cited at the beginning of this chapter: the concern regarding participat-

6. It is clear that the apostle at least implies if not actually expects that a single loaf of bread is used in the celebration of the Lord's Supper. Though there is no explicit reference to the cup, one cannot help but wonder if the apostle intended one loaf and one cup, critical and essential symbols of the unity within the community. Thus, the use of diced bread and trays of little, individual cups would seem to run counter to what is a nonnegotiable symbol of unity. This would suggest that even if, for logistical reasons, the use of small pieces of bread and small cups is necessary, at the very least a single loaf and a single cup should be clearly visible and central in the words of institution. Further, it is always appropriate to highlight that the single loaf represents the unity and common faith of those gathered.

ing in an unworthy manner, the need to examine oneself, and the need to "discern the body." These words are frequently read each time the Lord's Supper is observed, with the reminder that each person is to examine his or her conscience lest anyone participate "in an unworthy manner." For those who grew up with this passage as the sole or primary reading in connection with the Lord's Supper, it may be relatively easy to conclude that the Lord's Supper is a table of judgment—where we are reminded that we are unworthy because of the sin in our lives and that unless we deal with this sin we participate in a manner that is blamable and thus brings judgment on ourselves.

We certainly need to take sin seriously. Each person should examine his or her heart, and such self-examination is distinctly moralistic: We think of those things or attitudes that are less than good and confess them, thereby addressing what makes us unworthy of the Lord's Supper. Yet while there is much that is good in sober self-reflection, this emphasis all too easily leads to a distortion—a misreading—of the text.[7] The apostle Paul's intention was to address the abuse of the Lord's Supper. The Corinthian church was divided along socioeconomic lines, and, as Paul insists, this was inconsistent with the fundamental meaning of the event. The Lord's Supper was being held, as was almost all early Christian worship, in the homes of the wealthy. This was a necessity—the homes of the wealthy were large enough to hold a small congregation. But it created a potential problem. The owners of these homes would sometimes have private meals with their peers just before the celebration of the Lord's Supper, thereby emphasizing socioeconomic distinctions rather than unity within the Corinthian church community. It is likely that those who were not included in the private meal were actually seated separately. Thus, Paul declares that the common meal, the observance of the Lord's Supper in this context, was an abuse of the very meaning of the sacred event. The wealthy were hosting the Lord's Supper without regard to the whole body of Christ, highlighting differences rather than unity. They were, in effect, humiliating those who had nothing or little. They ate their fill, ignoring the poor, thereby doing more harm than good.

7. My reading of this text follows Gordon D. Fee, *The First Epistle to the Corinthians* (Grand Rapids: Eerdmans, 1987), 531–68.

In response, Paul reiterated the Lord's words of institution: The meal is in remembrance of Christ Jesus and proclaims his death. Paul then stressed that if we eat and drink in a manner that violates Christ and the body, we pass sentence on (make a judgment about) ourselves. Thus, the issue here is not whether we are worthy of partaking of the Lord's Supper. We are always unworthy. It is always by mercy that we come to this table. It is always a gift. Rather, the issue is whether the mode or manner of observation is worthy of the meaning of the event. It is not a question of introspective examination of the sin in our lives so that we become worthy. Rather, the critical question is whether we discern or recognize the body of believers with whom we have gathered. The reference to the body (1 Cor. 11:24) is likely an allusion to the elements themselves—shorthand for the body and blood of the Lord. However, the reference to the body also speaks of the community of faith. Paul is concerned that the believers are not recognizing their common identity as a body.

And so they were called to wait for one another (vv. 33–34) and to eat and drink in consideration of one another. If they wanted to eat together as peers or because they were hungry, they were to do so privately before they gathered to celebrate the Lord's Supper.

The Christian experience is one of being within a community as the body of Christ. Consequently, we celebrate this holy meal with reference to both the body of Christ—the incarnate One—and the body of Christ as the community of faith. The two are intimately linked. If we are not in fellowship with one another, we will not know the grace of being in fellowship with the incarnate, risen, and ascended Lord Jesus Christ.

It is unfortunate, then, that for so many the Lord's Supper has become little more than an occasion for a personal, moralized self-examination out of a sincere concern that we are sinners who need to be more holy. Such self-examination, as mentioned, usually takes place along the lines of behavior and attitude. The vision of holiness in the New Testament, however, is highly communal. Holiness is experienced as we grow up in Christ *together*. There is no holiness without unity in the body of Christ. The irony is that the very text of Scripture that calls for an appreciation of this unity has been turned on its head and used to cultivate an individualized, often legalistic, perspective on holiness. What makes the observance of the Lord's Supper unworthy is not so much moral failures as a lack of mutual fellowship and mutual regard. The great danger is that we are not at peace with one another.

Does this discount the need for personal examination? Not at all. We will come to this when we consider the Lord's Supper as a renewal of the covenant. The prior concern, however, is that we need to be in fellowship with one another. In other words, the basis for our fellowship with one another is not economic, social, or ethnic ties. It is not education or even our comradery and friendship. So often individuals resist the formalization of the Lord's Supper and insist that anyone anywhere can break bread with another. They assert that they can celebrate the Lord's Supper at home with their family or on a camping trip with their friends. What they fail to appreciate, though, is that in each case the basis of their "communion" is their familial tie or friendship—all well and good in itself but not the basis for *this* meal. Families should eat together; friends should prepare and eat meals together. This is vital to their identity as family and friends. But this eating together should not be called the Lord's Supper. We should call a meal the Lord's Supper only when the only possible basis for our eating together is our common identity in Jesus and our common communion with one another and with the living Christ.

The Lord's Supper is the meal of the church, the body of Christ, and our basis for gathering around this table is not our blood affiliation but the fact that we have been called together by Christ. This meal, in the language of the hymn "The Church's One Foundation," is the holy food of the faith community:

> Elect from every nation,
> Yet one o'er all the earth;
> Her charter of salvation,
> One Lord, one faith, one birth;
> One holy Name she blesses,
> Partakes one holy food,
> And to one hope she presses,
> With every grace endued.

I would press this point further. The basis of our gathering around this table should never be thought of in doctrinal terms—so that those with whom we fellowship at the Lord's Supper are those who agree with our reading of the biblical text or our particular theological or doctrinal heritage. In the Lord's Supper, we declare our unity not only with those immediately present, a particular gathering of Christians, but also with all Christians everywhere.

Each time we gather we do so on the assumption that all Christians are, as a matter of principle, welcome at this table, this observance. We "discern the body" (1 Cor. 11:29) each time we gather and celebrate the church catholic—women and men from every nation and tribe and language. We "discern the body" each time we welcome guests among us who come from other theological or denominational traditions. To exclude someone from the table because he or she is not of our denomination or church tradition is to fail to discern the body of Christ. Thus, a guest in our midst is a potent way in which we can demonstrate that our fellowship is with all Christians—represented by this guest in our company.[8]

Christ himself hosts us at this meal. In this event we are in fellowship with the Lord of glory. And in this event we are accepted by Christ as we welcome others even as Christ welcomed us (Rom. 15:7). Christ reminds us of his love and his peace and receives us afresh into his company. He draws us to one another, for in Christ there is no male or female, slave or free, Jew or Gentile (Gal. 3:28), east or west, rich or poor. All of this

---

8. This suggests that the only legitimate approach to the Lord's Supper is "open communion"; "closed communion" is an oxymoron. But it also suggests that there is no place for solitary communion. The Lord's Supper is, by its very nature, a corporate event—a meal of the community, not the individual. This is not to discount the place of personal, private prayer and a personal, intimate fellowship with Christ. It is rather to insist that this meal is an encounter with both Christ and the people of God. It is an act by which we are in fellowship with Christ and with others, and the two dimensions, of necessity, always go together. It is appropriate though for the elements of the Lord's Table to be taken to those who cannot be present with the community—those in prison or whose health makes it impossible for them to be present. But then the elements themselves come from the common gathering, and this is made clear both in the common event and in the smaller celebration. The second is derivative of the first.

anticipates the consummation of the kingdom when we will see Christ face-to-face and will gather from every tribe, tongue, and nation—Palestinian and Israeli, Irish Catholic and Irish Protestant, Tutu and Huti. We are all one in Christ. In the Lord's Supper, we experience a foretaste of this. More than anything else we say or do, the Lord's Supper enables us to receive the peace of Christ, to live in the peace of Christ, and to be a means by which the peace of Christ comes to our world.

5

FORGIVENESS

The Lord's Supper as a Table of Mercy

> While they were eating, Jesus took a loaf of bread, and after bless-ing it he broke it, gave it to the disciples, and said, "Take, eat; this is my body." Then he took a cup, and after giving thanks he gave it to them, saying, "Drink from it, all of you; for this is my blood of the covenant, which is poured out for many for the forgiveness of sins."
>
> Matthew 26:26–28

Historically, the church has wrestled with a question that has endured to the present when it comes to the observance of the Lord's Supper: Who is able to partake of the table and under what conditions? As mentioned in the previous chapter, many have been taught that this meal is an encounter with a holy God, and as such, it is a terrifying event and the occasion for reviewing the state of one's soul. The table is only for those who no longer live in sin. If a sinner participates, the table is desecrated. Thus, it is common for people not to partake because they feel that there is unresolved sin in their lives. The great fear of the consequences of "partaking unworthily" means that for some Christians this meal is dreaded and even avoided.

In my own upbringing, we were taught to examine ourselves lest we partake unworthily. Naturally, we never felt worthy! The perspective that the table is only for those who have addressed their sin was not new to my tradition. For example, in the sixteenth century, the Council of Trent established a requirement that Roman Catholics needed to take communion at least once a year. If they did not, they would be guilty of a mortal sin. The minimum was imposed because as a rule people were prepared to forego communion; it was not desired or entered into eagerly. It was feared as a table of judgment.

The concern with sanctity is legitimate, and the need for self-examination is appropriate. This will be addressed in the next chapter, which speaks of the Lord's Supper as an act of covenant renewal. However, something is profoundly out of place when this is *all* that is highlighted at the celebration of the Lord's Supper. Such an emphasis skews and distorts our understanding and our experience of Christ at this meal. The consequence is that all too easily the table is viewed as a place of judgment rather than as a table of mercy. With this perspective, the point of approaching the table is to "get right with God" rather than to live in God's love and faithfulness and the grace of an all-empowering gospel. In other words, the very core of the gospel and the meaning of the Lord's Supper are threatened. This is a meal in which sin is confronted, but the question is, When and how do we confront sin? Further, what posture of heart should we bring to the table?

First, we always come to this table as sinners in need of grace. Second, each celebration of the Lord's Supper is a fresh experience of the gospel, for at this table, our host, the Lord Jesus Christ, meets us with compassion and open arms. This is a table for sinners; this is a table of mercy. At this table, we both proclaim and actually experience the gospel. We find and experience forgiveness—the forgiveness out of which the whole of the Christian life can and must be lived.

Jesus as One Who Ate with Sinners

One of the most compelling aspects of the story of Jesus in the Gospels is that he consciously and intentionally chose to eat with sinners. Peter denied Jesus in the moments leading up to the crucifixion. Yet after the resurrection, we find Jesus making breakfast for this sinner in need of grace (John 21). This fundamental posture toward human failure was offensive to the religious teachers and authorities, Jesus' contemporaries, for they recognized that Jesus was accepting sinners and granting them forgiveness. They viewed this as an abomination, for it seemed to them that Jesus was taking sin lightly.

This is an absurd idea, of course. Jesus went to the cross because of sin, to bear the sins of all and to free people and communities and ultimately the entire world from the oppressive power of sin. Jesus did not take sin lightly. But he did have the conviction that healing and restoration are possible when we live our lives out of the empowering grace of his forgiveness. Judgmentalism and legalism are but another form of death. In Jesus, sin is confronted with compassion and mercy, and this is the only posture that can ultimately lead to authentic transformation. We are to be empowered by the gospel to be new people.

Jesus ate with sinners, and Jesus responded with compassion to sinners—another compelling feature of the Gospels. Filled with compassion, we read in Mark 1, Jesus reached out and healed a leprous man. In both Matthew and Mark, we read that Jesus was filled with compassion when he saw the hunger of the people; they were like sheep without a shepherd. What is notable in these Gospel accounts is that Jesus fed them. He hosted meals. In the amazing account of Zacchaeus, the man of Luke 19, Jesus meets him on the road to Jericho and announces, indeed declares, in the wonderful words of the song we sang as children, "I'm coming to your house for tea!" The religious leaders grumbled, "He has gone to be the guest of one who is a sinner" (v. 7). This is but an echo of their earlier complaint about Jesus: "This fellow welcomes sinners and eats with them" (Luke 15:2).

Jesus ate with sinners. He did so not because he tolerated sin but as an act of compassion, an act that he knew to be the only possible way he could respond to sinners and empower them to move from sin to salvation, from sin to righteousness. We simply do not appreciate the gospel or that the Lord's Table is a proclamation of the gospel unless we live in this reality. Thus, each time the church gathers at the holy meal, it is another occasion to show that we come as sinners to the table of mercy and are received by the one who opens his arms in compassion. As such, it is an event in which we anticipate what is yet to come, the marriage supper of the Lamb at the consummation of the kingdom. We will be received at this meal, and the basis of admission is nothing but the mercy of Christ. We will be taken up in the wideness of Christ's mercy.

In anticipation of that day, we celebrate the Lord's Supper now as an act of remembrance, as an occasion for fellowship with Christ and one another, and as an opportunity to appropriate afresh the forgiveness of God so that we can live in the world free of guilt and condemnation. It is a meal to which we come recognizing that we have sinned yet again in thought, word, and deed and must appropriate the forgiveness of God, which frees us from guilt and empowers us to live in the light.

Therefore, this is the table at which forgiveness is both celebrated and experienced. We gather at this table as forgiven sinners to receive once more God's forgiveness in Christ. Only as we know forgiveness can we hope to turn from sin. We must come to the table of mercy, then, with eagerness. As we come, we pray, "Christ have mercy." We lift up our hearts to the Lamb of God, who was slain for the sins of the world, particularly for our sins. And as we come, Jesus says to us, in the words of Matthew 26:27–28, "Drink from it, all of you; for this is my blood of the covenant, which is poured out for many for the forgiveness of sins."

The Faithfulness of Christ

When the church speaks of this meal as a celebration of the blood of Christ, "poured out for many for the forgiveness of sins," it is extolling the faithfulness of Christ—*his* obedience that took him to the cross. It is easy for us to come to this holy meal with a grave concern about our own level of faithfulness. The sad fact is that we have been taught to do this. We are called to introspection and self-examination and urged to see how we have not been nearly as faithful as we should have been or could have been. The problem is that then the primary focus of our attention in coming to the meal is our own faith or lack thereof, our own faithfulness or lack thereof. The Lord's Supper becomes self-centered instead of Christ-centered.

This is an event in which first and foremost we celebrate and affirm the faithfulness of Christ, who acted on our behalf and on whose faithfulness we now depend. We look to Jesus, who is the author of our faith and the one through whom the salvation of God is made known. The Lord's Supper is not celebrated as an event of the gospel unless we remember that Jesus hosts this event and welcomes us into fellowship with him and with one another. Jesus the crucified Lord has given his life for us so that through his shed blood we can experience the forgiveness of sins. This meal is only about us insofar as it is first about Jesus.

If we are saved, it is on account of the faithfulness of Jesus. This does not discount the need for our repentance and response to the faithfulness of Christ. We come as repentant sinners eager to know that we are forgiven, but we know this, in the end, not by the exercise of our will or our faithfulness but because of the faithfulness of the living Christ.

Can We Speak of the Lord's Supper as a Sacrifice?

A number of debates over the centuries have created serious divisions in the Christian community when it comes to the understanding and practice of this sacred event—including, of course, whether Christ is truly present at the celebration and who can appropriately take part in this celebration. But a third question has been equally vexing to the church: Can we speak of the Lord's Supper as a *sacrifice*?

We can certainly speak of the Lord's Supper as an act of self-offering—specifically, the sacrifice of ourselves through praise and thanksgiving. Indeed, we are living sacrifices (Rom. 12:1). In this way we enter into the fellowship that is already within the Holy Trinity; we make our offering *to* the Father, *through* the Son, by the *enabling* of the Spirit.

But where the division comes is in whether it is appropriate to speak of the Lord's Supper as a *sacrifice* of Christ. Can we speak of the sacramental presence of the cross and of how in the Lord's Supper Christ's sacrifice is made present to participants? Can we speak of an immediacy of the sacrifice of Christ on the cross such that in our celebration we are entering intimately into the grace that the cross represents, especially the grace of forgiveness? If we can speak of the Lord's Supper as a sacrifice, then the Lord's Supper enables us to be not merely observers but actual participants in the sacrifice of Christ Jesus.

The issue as to whether there is a sacrificial element to the Lord's Supper has been very divisive for the church, with strong views on both sides. On the one hand, some emphasize the *finished* work of Christ. Therefore, the Lord's Supper cannot in any way, shape, or form be viewed as a "renewed" sacrifice. The sacrifice of Christ is "once for all," they insist, noting the language of Hebrews 9:28. On the whole, this has been the emphasis of Protestant theological traditions. This insistence on the all sufficiency of Christ has often led to an even greater insistence that the Lord's Supper is only a memorial, an exercise of looking back to the finished work of Christ, something that happened in the past that cannot be supplemented. The Lord's Supper, then, looks back to the cross in the past tense; it is not a present tense experience of the crucified Christ.

The counterargument comes from those who take note of the language of Paul in Colossians 1:24, where he speaks of suffering what is lacking in the sufferings of Christ. This perspective, found most commonly within high Anglican, Roman Catholic, and Eastern Orthodox traditions, insists that the Christian church can even now mystically experience the suffering of Christ on the cross, that the sacrifice of Christ is dynamically and experientially present to the church today, and that this is most obviously the case during the celebration of the Lord's Supper. Thus, there is the implicit understanding within the Roman tradition, which so horrified Martin Luther, that in the celebration of the mass, Christ is sacrificed in the hands of the one presiding at the altar.

Martin Luther and the Reformers recoiled at the idea of a resacrifice. Their insistence on the sufficient and complete work of Christ left them incapable of accepting that the Lord's Supper is a sacrifice. They were convinced that the medieval notion of sacrifice in the mass failed to preserve the uniqueness of the cross as the sufficiency of Christ's offering in response to the human predicament.

The solution they proposed, however, created another problem—that at the Lord's Supper a Christian enters into the sacrifice of Jesus only in a purely cognitive way. The problem is ably captured by Dom Gregory Dix in his classic work on liturgy and worship published in 1945. He highlights the contrast between the Roman Church and the Reformers and notes that there is a "logical and inevitable development from the protestant bias," namely, that the Eucharist is entered into in a solely mental manner, wherein we are reminded of something that is no longer present. Thus, "the real eucharistic action (if 'action' is not a misleading term) takes place mentally, in the isolated secrecy of the individual's mind . . . [and it] goes on separately, even if simultaneously, within each man's mind. . . . Further this means that the external rite is no longer a *corporate* rite integral to the performance of the eucharist action, but a common preparation for it, designed only to prepare each communicant subjectively to perform it for himself." Therefore, he concludes, "there is no way of entering into Christ's action . . . by a mere mental remembering of it, however rigid or devout."[1]

In other words, we seem forced to choose between a *repetition* of Calvary and a purely subjective, mental, and highly individual remembering of a past event no longer present, which leaves us merely spectators of the cross of Christ rather than participants in the work of Christ.

I have seen the effects of this again and again in evangelical Protestant circles. The minister urges those who are present to use the occasion to *think about* the death of Jesus. We are typically urged to remember, to look back and realize what has been done for us and to do so in a manner that would cultivate a deep appreciation in us. The hoped-for outcome of this thinking is that we would become more grateful and more faithful in the manner of our living. But something profound is missing in this equation. It is purely an individual experience; each one does his or her own thinking, an internal, personal process. Further, any benefit in the celebration of the Lord's Supper rests on our

1. Cited in C. F. D. Moule, *Forgiveness and Reconciliation* (London: SPCK, 1998), 168–69.

capacity to think, to exercise our wills, to be as faithful as we can. There is nothing to look to and lean on other than what we can conjure up in our minds.

But there is a way forward, a resolution to the dilemma, expressed in two assertions.[2] First, the work of Christ is finished and does not need to be supplemented or repeated. Second, and just as important, Paul speaks of finishing what is lacking in the work of Christ. In so doing, Paul portrays the experience of the union with Christ in his death and resurrection—a dynamic, present-day union between believers and the power of Christ's work in their lives. What is lacking is the full experience of what Christ has done. Christians, in their sufferings, are joint heirs with Christ in his sufferings (Rom. 8:17). And their sufferings with Christ are a vital means by which they experience the sanctifying grace of God, the completion of Christ's work. Thus, the definitive work of Christ (once for all) is also a continuous act by which Christians appropriate what it means to live in dynamic and mystical union with the crucified and risen Christ.

The Lord's Supper bespeaks the continuous appropriation of the benefits of the cross in the life of the church. When we offer our obedience in the Lord's Supper, we do so as an act of identification with the obedience of Christ. But our approach to God is always in, through, and with the crucified and risen Christ, the one in whom we live and move and have our being. We are united with him in his suffering and death so that we might be united with him in his resurrection (1 Pet. 4:13).

In other words, we do not re-crucify Christ. We do not repeat the crucifixion during the Lord's Supper. But we are crucified *with* him. His sacrifice is repeated in the sense that we identify with it so intimately and immediately that it becomes a dynamic reality in our lives. As C. F. D. Moule puts its, "Every Eucharist is a 'focal' point of [Christ's sacrifice]; not a mere recalling to the mind, nor yet a re-enactment; but an entering into what Christ has done—just as indeed is every symbol of obedience."[3]

As such, the Lord's Supper is a real, actual *koinonia* with Christ's body and blood. It happens in real time, in the here and

---

2. In what follows, I am relying on the argument of C. F. D. Moule in a 1956 piece republished in *Forgiveness and Reconciliation*.

3. Ibid., 171.

now, as we, the people of God, eat this meal together. Consider also the way in which Wolfhart Pannenberg expresses this:

> The celebration of the Lord's Supper cannot be the church's sacrifice in the sense of the offering to God on the altar, by the hands of a human priest, of a holy gift different from ourselves. It can be only the entry of the church into the self-giving of Christ, i.e., the offering of ourselves, by, with, and in Jesus Christ, as a living sacrifice in the signs of bread and wine. For nothing effects participation in the body and blood of Christ but entering into that which we receive.[4]

Therefore, when we come to the holy meal, we entrust ourselves to Christ. We are not looking to the priest or the pastor to reenact or reperform a sacrifice. We are not hoping that as best as we can we will be able to recall the death of Jesus in our own hearts and minds. Rather, we let Jesus carry the day. As we remember him, he is the risen Lord who is present and who by his Spirit draws us into his work on the cross. The Spirit enables us in the Lord's Supper to enter into the sacrifice of Jesus not so much in our heads as in our actual eating and drinking. We are participants in what is happening as we embrace the symbols of the bread and the cup. We do not need to strain our minds and our imaginations to see beyond the elements, assuming that what really counts is our thinking. Rather, we can just eat and drink!

Forgiving Others as We Have Been Forgiven

When we eat and drink, in faith trusting in the work of Christ, who is present in our midst, through God's mercy we experience the grace of forgiveness. We do not simply choose to believe that we are forgiven; rather, we experience the forgiveness of God. As we do, we are then empowered to forgive others, beginning with those with whom we are celebrating this meal. The table is never merely about our forgiveness. It is also about the forgiveness

---

4. Wolfhart Pannenberg, *Systematic Theology*, vol. 3, trans. Geoffrey W. Bromiley (Grand Rapids: Eerdmans, 1998), 317.

we offer to others. In other words, the Lord's Supper enables us to live the gospel, to embody what it means to be a people who are transformed by the good news.

At the Lord's Supper, then, we celebrate and declare the mercy of God; we proclaim that forgiveness is found in Christ. But more, in the Lord's Supper we also experience this grace. We thus gather at this event as forgiven sinners alongside other forgiven sinners who are learning the grace of mutual forgiveness. God's forgiveness is a particular expression of the love of God. Thus, the Lord's Supper is first and foremost an encounter with God's love. As St. Francis de Sales counseled, "Your great intention in receiving Communion should be to advance, strengthen, and comfort yourself in the love of God."[5] This dynamic—an awareness of God's love, known in God's forgiveness—becomes an experience of the gospel that, in turn, enables us to grow in faith, hope, and love.

5. St. Francis de Sales, *Introduction to the Devout Life,* trans. John K. Ryan (New York: Doubleday, 1950), 108.

6

COVENANT

The Lord's Supper as a Renewal of Baptismal Vows

While they were eating, he took a loaf of bread, and after blessing it he broke it, gave it to them, and said, "Take; this is my body." Then he took a cup, and after giving thanks he gave it to them, and all of them drank from it. He said to them, "This is my blood of the covenant, which is poured out for many. Truly I tell you, I will never again drink of the fruit of the vine until that day when I drink it new in the kingdom of God."

Mark 14:22–25

It is essential that we speak of the Lord's Supper as the renewal of a covenant. When we use the language of "covenant" in speaking of the Lord's Supper, we focus on the ethical significance of this holy meal and attend to how it enables us to be aligned with the kingdom purposes of God in the world. In a sense, the words we have considered thus far bring us into the event of the Lord's Supper *from* the world. We come out of the world to remember, to enter into fellowship with God and one another, and to be anchored afresh in the mercy and forgiveness of God. Now, out of this encounter with Christ, we anticipate our return to the world—to our relationships and our work.

When we speak of the link between the Lord's Supper and our lives in the world, two words inform our thinking. Both are found in the words of institution in the Gospel of Mark, and both are central to our appreciation of this event in the life of God's people. The two words are *kingdom* and *covenant*. Both words are linked with the cup in Mark's Gospel. The words of institution in Matthew are slightly different, with the inclusion of the line "for the forgiveness of sins" not found in Mark's Gospel. In Mark, what is profiled is the reality of covenant renewal and the link with the kingdom of God. I am not suggesting that this is unique to Mark. Each account identifies the cup as the seal of the (new) covenant (Matt. 26:28; Luke 22:20; 1 Cor. 11:25), just as Moses sealed the covenant on Mount Sinai with the blood of an animal (Exod. 24:8). Mark's version, however, provides the opportunity to consider the link between the covenant and our identity as a people of a new commonwealth under the reign of God.

Each of the various words of institution emphasizes that a shedding of blood signifies atonement and the forgiveness of sins. But what it also implied in the language of the cup is that in and through the shed blood of Christ something is established for those who participate: They have a new identity, and as new people of God, they are called into a distinctive way of being in the world. The Lord's Supper is one of the most significant ways in which this new identity is profiled, expressly because of the intimate link between the covenant and the kingdom. Thus, both words are an essential window or lens through which we understand the work of God in our world, and both words belong to the language and thought categories of the ancient world.

The Kingdom of God

Jesus frequently spoke of the kingdom: "Truly I tell you, I will never again drink of the fruit of the vine until that day when I drink it new in the kingdom of God" (Mark 14:25). In so doing, he made it plain that salvation through the cross ultimately finds expression in the reign of Christ. The basic assumption behind this idea is that freedom is found where there is justice and peace and that justice and peace embrace under the authority of Christ. Authority, then, is not a negative or pejorative term; it speaks, rather, of hope and freedom. What we long for, in the words of the Lord's Prayer, is that "thy will [may] be done on earth as it is in heaven . . . for yours is the kingdom and the power and the glory."

Humanity lost its moorings when it chose to go its own way. What the language of the kingdom highlights is that freedom is found through submission to the authority and will of God. We trust God and live in obedience to his will. Justice and peace result when Christ rules as king, as Lord.

The crisis of our world is that there is a false prince at large, one whose rule is based on oppression and lies. What we long for is that the Prince of Peace would once more reign on the throne of the universe.

Jesus came to establish the kingdom of God, to defeat and destroy the powers of darkness, and to bring truth, justice, and peace to our world. Romans 8 declares that the whole of creation groans in anticipation of the day when this will happen, when Christ will be revealed as Lord of the cosmos.

In the meantime, the Christian community is a living witness to the reign of Christ. Even though justice and peace are yet to embrace in this world, the community of faith lives with the abiding conviction that we can even now live under the reign of Christ. When we do, it is an assault on the powers of darkness, a tangible sign of confidence that Jesus will one day make all things well and that even now he can rule in our hearts. Our lives, therefore, can be a foretaste of the kingdom that is yet to come.

Christians believe that despite what they see around them, Christ is on the throne of the universe. Christians sing hymns of praise, affirm their common faith, hear Christ speak to them through the Word, and receive Christ's Spirit to live as Christ's people in this world. They are the people of a new order, and this is reflected in a particular way of being in the world evident in the quality of their relationships, the character of their work, and their identification in word and deed with the reign of Christ in the world.

People of the Covenant

What marks the community of faith is that these people have entered into a covenant relationship. The covenant speaks of the mode or method by which God enters into a relationship with his people and also of what it means to live in light of the kingdom. The covenant is based on a promise. As it was put to Israel, "I will be your God, and you will be my people." The terms of the covenant are determined by God. God takes the initiative, establishes the parameters, and, in the end, guarantees the covenant—that those who enter into it will experience what is promised, the salvation and blessing of God.

The new covenant that Jesus establishes with his disciples is clearly in continuity with the old covenant established through Moses with the people of Israel. In using the language of blood sacrifice in Mark 14, Jesus recalls the Mosaic covenant (Exod. 24:3–8) and the blood of the bulls that was shed. Now Jesus establishes a covenant with his disciples through his own blood, and through this covenant he invites them to live under his authority and reign. Their obedience will be in faith because Christ will not be physically present. Though believers today do not see him, they believe in him and walk in obedience under his authority, thereby living by the terms of the covenant.

All covenants, whether between two people, as in a marriage, or between citizens and their government leader, or more specifically, between the church and its Lord and Savior, are represented and formalized through symbolic acts. Whether it is a ring or a handshake, a symbol not only calls a covenant to mind but actually establishes it. In the older language of the marriage ceremony, "With this ring I thee wed," the symbol effects the reality. A covenant is established through the placement of a ring on a finger.

In the case of the church, there are two fundamental and central acts by which we are marked as the kingdom people of God, people of the covenant: baptism and the Lord's Supper. Through baptism—a formal rite of initiation—we represent and symbolize our identity in Christ, as those who die with him and rise with him (Rom. 6:1–6). This has immediate ethical significance, for as Paul stresses in Romans 6, sin is inconsistent with our baptismal identity. He goes on in this chapter to explain that we are no longer slaves to sin but slaves to righteousness.

Baptism, then, is a symbolic act or gesture by which we establish our identification with the kingdom of God. It is an act whereby we enter into the covenant that God has with his people. We communicate that we are the people of God. The terms of the covenant are simple: to trust and to obey. We must walk by faith, a faith that is evident in the quality and character of our lives. Despite everything we see around us, in trial and in the face of temptation, our baptism is our declaration that we choose to walk in the light, even in this dark world.

Such a declaration should be evident in our behavior and attitudes. For example, our God is not our money; we trust not in money but in Christ, who providentially cares for us. Therefore, we are free from anxiety and worry and free to live in integrity and generosity. We are free also from the eroticism of our culture, free to walk in the truth as those who know that sexuality is a gift given within the covenant relationship of marriage, and to know that this makes sexuality holy and whole. We are free to speak the truth in love, to speak with integrity, to choose speech and words that honor, dignify, and affirm. We do not need to hide behind words; we do not need to patronize or manipulate with words.

Our declaration means that we do not live in fear. We are a people who against all the evidence choose to trust in Jesus and to live our lives in obedience to him. We are people of the new covenant. And we are not alone. We make this resolve together as the community of faith.

The Holy Meal and the Renewal of the Covenant

It is through a meal that Jesus establishes and sustains the covenant he has with his followers, enabling them to live under his reign, the kingdom of God. He proclaims that this covenant is established in his blood shed on the cross, but he also gives us an act or means by which to confirm the covenant and to renew our identity within that covenant: the Lord's Supper. Baptism is the rite of initiation, the act that establishes our identity as participants in the covenant, as those who with the Christian

71

community choose to live under the reign of God. The Lord's Supper, in turn, is the rite—the tangible corporate act—by which the terms of our baptism are renewed and sustained in our lives. Every time we come to this table, we partake in remembrance of Christ's death, of the establishing of the covenant through the shed blood of Jesus. We come to the table of mercy to receive once more forgiveness for the many ways in which we have failed to live as people of the kingdom. But this table is also the place where the covenant is renewed.

Each time we come to the table we establish our identity as the people of God, people who are alien to this world and its values. We come for a realignment of our lives with our confession of faith. In our worship, we declare in our confession, prayers, and hymns that we are the people of God. At the Lord's Table, we establish once again this identity through the very means that have been given to us by Christ. We experience the renewal of the covenant he has given us and established with us.

It would appear that no Christian theological and spiritual tradition emphasized this theme—the Lord's Supper as a renewal of the covenant—as did the seventeenth- and eighteenth-century Puritans. This is evident, for example, in the writings of Edmund Calamy (1600–1666), a Puritan prominent in the Westminster Assembly whose main work was the preparation of the Westminster Confession, a defining document for Puritan Calvinism.[1] Calamy emphasizes that the Lord's Supper is a federal ordinance[2] and that this necessarily implies a covenant transaction. This, for Calamy, is the main thing that happens in the celebration of this meal. He speaks of those Christians who in the celebration of the Lord's Supper "endeavour to think affectionately of His incarnation, passion and crucifixion; and thus far indeed 'tis well. But when they stop here and go no further, they leave out the main thing."[3]

1. The following is based on two essays by Calamy that are representative of the Puritan perspective on the Lord's Supper. Both are found in Don Kistler, ed., *The Puritans and the Lord's Supper* (Morgan, PA: Soli Deo Gloria Publications, 1997).

2. That is, a matter between a membership and its authority.

3. Kistler, *Puritans and the Lord's Supper,* 24.

The Puritan authors remind their readers that it was an ancient Hebrew custom to renew a covenant at a meal, to eat and drink in the presence of God, as was evident, in particular, in the peace offerings. This pledge at a meal speaks of an oath, the original meaning of the word *sacrament*. Thus, the commemoration involves a renewal of the oath. In other words, "every time we come to the Lord's Table, we must vow and engage that we'll continue as Christ's faithful servants, subjects, and soldiers, and never do anything against His crown and dignity as long as we live."[4]

Calamy goes on to stress that the benefits of the Lord's Supper and the extent to which this meal is a means by which we grow in grace are in some measure determined by whether we approach the table and experience the Lord's Supper as a renewal of the covenant. We must come to the table seeking and anticipating that we will experience a strengthening of our resolve, a renewal of our hope, and an increased measure of comfort.[5]

All of this suggests that we must be sober minded and appreciate the gravity of what we are doing. Calamy urges his readers not to take the event of the Lord's Supper lightly. No doubt this Puritan heritage has led many contemporary evangelical congregations to approach the Lord's Supper as though it were a funeral, something of great weight and gravity in which believers participate not just with soberness but with somberness, an almost dark sense of foreboding. In doing so, the sense they often get is of their great failures as Christians and thus that they are deeply unworthy to participate. Here Calamy offers a good corrective by warning that while we must be serious—this is a covenant renewal—we must beware of an "over-great scrupulosity," a perfectionism that does not accept human "infirmities."[6]

The Covenant, the Kingdom, and Christian Mission

The Puritans appropriately viewed the Lord's Table as an occasion for moral realignment. In this event, Christians, individually

4. Ibid., 36.
5. Ibid., 38–39.
6. Ibid., 46.

and as a community, identify with the marks of the Christian faith. But recent reflections on the Lord's Supper have rightly complemented this call to personal moral reform with the need to see this as a renewal of all that we are called to be in the world. It is a moral reordering, but it is also a realignment with the kingdom purposes of God. Thus, it is linked intimately with the prayer, "Thy will be done on earth as it is in heaven."

The Lord's Supper, therefore, is not an escape from the world and from our missional and social responsibility in and for the world. Neither is it a withdrawal into a world of subjective piety. It is specifically an act by which we are enabled to discern the world, to see and to respond in a manner that is consistent with the reign of God. Our vision for the world is renewed, and we are reoriented with the will and purposes of God. Indeed, if participation in the Lord's Supper does not foster a capacity to see and act with courage, integrity, love, and justice in the world, then the holy meal is in danger of becoming nothing more than a form of communal self-indulgence. It must be an event that turns us back to a thoughtful and courageous engagement with the world.

On the one hand, it is imperative that we appreciate the close connection that exists between the Lord's Supper and Christian mission. This is the meal of the kingdom, a tangible sign for those who participate that they believe that Christ Jesus has come to establish a kingdom of justice and peace. It only follows that not all who could or should be at the table are indeed there. Whether it is a large congregation or a small gathering of believers who break bread, the Lord's Supper reminds us that there are many who are not yet at the table. Thus, the event calls for mission—the proclamation of the good news, the eager and informed invitation to all to come to the table, to meet the host of the meal, and to experience his transforming grace. Mission naturally flows from the celebration of the Lord's Supper.

In a similar fashion, this meal calls to mind the Christian responsibility for social justice. Gustavo Gutierrez rightly insists that the Eucharist is an act of identification with those present but also with the suffering and those who cry for political liberation and socioeconomic justice. "Without a real commitment," he writes, "against exploitation and alienation and for a society

74

of solidarity and justice, the Eucharist celebration is an empty action."[7]

Thus, the Lord's Supper involves a conscious and deliberate act of identification with God's kingdom purposes in the world. In this event, there is both the motivation and the grace to be all that we are called to be, to witness in word and deed to the very gospel that is portrayed in this meal. We move from table fellowship to the ministry of reconciliation.

Implicit in the celebration, therefore, is a call to service. It is ironic that at the Last Supper the disciples debated who was greatest among them (Luke 22:24–27). What a discussion given the occasion! In response, Jesus declared that he was among them as one who serves. Jesus' act of washing the feet of his disciples is a tangible reminder that in this meal believers are also called and empowered for mission and service. Through this event, we identify with Christ and embrace the grace to be in the world as those who serve.

This necessarily means that there is a close connection between the Lord's Supper and the sufferings of Christ and the sufferings of those who choose to follow him. In the Lord's Supper, we identify with the Suffering Servant and turn to embrace the suffering of the world. There is an intimate and close affinity between sacrament and suffering.

Who Then Is Welcome at the Table?

All of this has implications for an abiding question when it comes to the practice of the Lord's Supper: Who is welcome at

7. Gustavo Gutierrez, *A Theology of Liberation: History, Politics, and Salvation,* trans. and ed. Sister Caridad Inda and John Eagleson (Maryknoll, NY: Orbis, 1973), 265. Other noteworthy contributions are Monika Hellwig, *The Eucharist and World Hunger* (New York: Paulist Press, 1976); and Joseph A. Grassi, *Broken Bread and Broken Bodies: The Lord's Supper and World Hunger* (Maryknoll, NY: Orbis, 1985). I should note, though, that Gutierrez insists that the oppressor must cease to oppress before being welcomed at the table. But as Lesslie Newbigin stresses in *The Open Secret,* "It is a very perilous responsibility which is taken by a man who makes such a judgment," and the "Eucharist is the point at which we acknowledge the fact that we are all in sin and that we are accepted only by grace" ([Grand Rapids: Eerdmans, 1978], 123, 124). More will be said on this later in this chapter when we ask the question, Who is welcome at the table?

this table? Further, on what basis, if any, is a person excluded from participation? These are not easy or straightforward questions, and one can find a spectrum of responses across the contemporary Christian community. For some, to participate one must be a baptized member of that particular church denomination; for others, all that is needed is that one is baptized in the name of the Father, Son, and Spirit—even if within another denomination. For still others, all that is needed is the self-authentication that a person has received Jesus as his or her Savior and Lord, as is typically stated within evangelical communities (no one else needs to corroborate this, and often even baptism is not required). In yet other communities, a radical openness is practiced, such that all are welcome and no one is excluded from the table.

For some traditions, this issue is made more complicated when the Lord's Supper becomes the focal point of church discipline. Within the U.S. Roman Catholic Church, for example, there was considerable debate leading up to the 2004 election as to whether public officials, particularly candidates for election, should be barred from communion when their votes in Congress go against church teachings. In other settings, it is not so much church teachings that are in question but a person's behavior. Should a person be admitted to the Lord's Supper if his or her behavior does not reflect a commitment to moral renewal and reform?

This dilemma—who is welcome (or not welcome) at the table—is graphically illustrated in the experience of Jonathan Edwards, Puritan, eighteenth-century New England preacher, and theologian. The New England Puritans had many intense debates on this subject, seeking to determine who should have access to the communion table, and Edwards was caught up in the midst of it. Solomon Stoddard, Edwards's grandfather, called for open communion. He insisted that it was too hard to know who was truly converted. We cannot, he said, read or discern the heart of another. Further, the Lord's Supper, he believed, was a converting ordinance and a means of grace that might actually foster conversion.[8]

---

8. George M. Marsden, *Jonathan Edwards: A Life* (New Haven: Yale University Press, 2003), 30–31.

Edwards instead followed his father, Timothy, and eventually was forced out of his pastoral appointment because he came to the conviction, an unpopular position in East Windsor, Connecticut, where he was serving as a pastor, that the table should be reserved for those who truly demonstrated that they were converted. In other words, he came to the conclusion that whereas a step-by-step conversion narrative may not be required, surely more than simple ascent was needed. Thus, he felt justified in asking for what he called a "credible profession."[9]

It was precisely the perspective that the Lord's Supper is a renewal of the covenant that shaped this conviction. For Edwards, the Lord's Supper is essentially a sign and a seal "renewing and confirming the covenant."[10] On the one hand, this led him to advocate the practice of weekly communion. Christians need a frequent renewal of the covenant, he insisted. But it also signified for Edwards that this is a "solemn covenant ceremony."[11] He denounced hypocrisy—any participation that did not include this sober appreciation of the character of the Lord's Supper—and insisted that only the truly converted could be welcomed at the table.

Edwards needs to be commended for his resolve; he probably had good reason to be distressed about the approach taken by his grandfather—perhaps even shocked at what he witnessed. Something is indeed amiss when participation in the Lord's Supper seemingly has no effect on a person's moral behavior. The sacrament is not merely a personal, individual act; the community of faith comes to the table together as a holy community to participate in a holy meal that in turn empowers the community to identify with the reign of God. If this is flouted or ignored by one or more participants, then all are affected.

Conversely, though, there is something valuable in the perspective of those who insist that we should welcome whosoever would come to the table. This is based largely on how Jesus approached those with whom he ate. Jesus intentionally ate with those at the margins—outcasts and tax collectors—as an act of compassion but also of empowerment. By doing so, he proclaimed the in-breaking of the kingdom. Such meals were integral to his mission, for they

9. Ibid., 347.
10. Ibid., 353.
11. Ibid., 354.

celebrated what God was already doing and what God would do. They were demonstrations of the inclusive love of God. Meals with Jesus were not reserved only for those who demonstrated an adequate level of holiness or sanctity.

Thus, it is noteworthy that John Wesley spoke of the Lord's Supper as a *converting sacrament*, pointing out that for many their first experience of the love of God and their first sense that they are sinners in need of grace come during the celebration of the Lord's Supper. Wesley was convinced that the table would meet a person in a manner congruent with his or her need. He writes, "Inasmuch as we come to his Table, not to give him anything, but to receive whatever he sees best for us, there is no previous preparation indispensably necessary, but a desire to receive whatsoever he pleases to give."[12]

There will certainly be times when a community determines that it simply cannot accept someone at the table; the person's life, work, and relationships are an affront to the gospel and to the fundamental values of that community. But this should happen only in extreme cases. The rule of thumb, it would seem, is that we err on the side of generosity. Our approach to the table should be not to set up barriers but to welcome and invite. Our words of institution should be eager and welcoming rather than ready reminders to non-Christians that this is not for them. This is not our table, which we are responsible to guard; it is the table of the Lord, where he offers himself and the grace of forgiveness. Further, Jesus himself invites those who participate to walk in the light, the light of the kingdom, under the covenant of grace. Our challenge as Christian communities, then, is to come to this table seeking to maintain two perspectives: At this table, we celebrate the unconditional love of God, and at this table, we are intentionally aligning ourselves with the kingdom of God.

The Covenant Written on the Heart

The words in the New Testament speak of the cup as the sign of the covenant. Luke 22:20 and 1 Corinthians 11:25 speak of the

---

12. Philip S. Watson, *The Message of the Wesleys: A Reader of Instruction and Devotion* (Grand Rapids: Francis Asbury Press, 1984), 137.

new covenant. It is noteworthy that the Old Testament context for this phrase is Jeremiah 31:31–33, where the prophet speaks of the need for the covenant to be written on the hearts of his hearers. His concern is that the covenant is not merely an external form but an inner reality, something that has formed and reformed their deepest affections, loyalties, and commitments. The new covenant would be established through Christ Jesus.

This is surely what we long for—an inner reform and transformation in which the full force and power of the gospel alter our most fundamental way of being. We are a people who live the gospel, whose hearts, minds, and wills are intimately linked with the values and perspective of the kingdom.

This will not happen without a resolve of the will, a personal commitment of the kind spoken of by the apostle Paul when he urges his readers to present themselves as a living sacrifice to God (Rom. 12:1). When we speak in this way, we are right to speak of Word and Spirit and to affirm the power of Scripture, preached and read in the grace of the Spirit, to bring about personal renewal and transformation. But we must not underestimate the formative capacity of the Lord's Supper. Many Christian traditions insist that the Word ultimately accomplishes its end, enabling us to grow in faith, hope, and love as we receive it as embodied souls, taking it right into our bodies. The reception of the transforming Word, by which our minds are renewed, is not merely a mental exercise. It is an act of the whole person. We receive the Word, feed on the Word, allow the Word to dwell within us (Col. 3:16). Thus, at the Lord's Supper we hear the Word and we eat and drink at the holy table as a tangible response to the preached Word and to the living, risen Christ, whose Word now takes form in our lives through the grace of the Spirit. The new covenant is written on our hearts.

7

NOURISHMENT

The Lord's Supper as Bread from Heaven

Jesus said to them, "I am the bread of life. Whoever comes to me will never be hungry, and whoever believes in me will never be thirsty. But I said to you that you have seen me and yet do not believe. Everything that the Father gives me will come to me, and anyone who comes to me I will never drive away; for I have come down from heaven, not to do my own will, but the will of him who sent me. And this is the will of him who sent me, that I should lose nothing of all that he has given me, but raise it up on the last day. This is indeed the will of my Father, that all who see the Son and believe in him may have eternal life; and I will raise them up on the last day."

Then the Jews began to complain about him because he said, "I am the bread that came down from heaven." They were saying, "Is not this Jesus, the son of Joseph, whose father and mother we know? How can he now say, 'I have come down from heaven'?" Jesus answered them, "Do not complain among yourselves. No one can come to me unless drawn by the Father who sent me; and I will raise that person up on the last day. It is written in the prophets, 'And they shall all be taught by God.' Everyone who has heard and learned from the Father comes to me. Not that anyone has seen the Father except the one who is from God; he has seen the Father. Very truly, I tell you, whoever believes has eternal life. I am the bread of life. Your ancestors ate the manna in the wilderness, and they died. This is the bread that comes down from heaven, so that one may eat of it and not die. I am the living bread that came down from heaven. Whoever eats of this bread will live forever; and the bread that I will give for the life of the world is my flesh."

The Jews then disputed among themselves, saying, "How can this man give us his flesh to eat?" So Jesus said to them, "Very truly, I tell you, unless you eat the flesh of the Son of Man and drink his blood, you have no life in you. Those who eat my flesh and drink my blood have eternal life, and I will raise them up on the last day; for my flesh is true food and my blood is true drink. Those who eat my flesh and drink my blood abide in me, and I in them. Just as the living Father sent me, and I live because of the Father, so whoever eats me will live because of me. This is the bread that came down from heaven, not like that which your ancestors ate, and they died. But the one who eats this bread will live forever."

John 6:35–58

We come now to a consideration of what it means to speak of the Lord's Supper as *spiritual food*. First, I want to explain the theological logic of the order in which I consider these dimensions of meaning. Our celebration of this meal is anchored in a past event that we remember and that as a past event is made present to us by virtue of the resurrection. Now Christ himself hosts a meal in which we are in fellowship with him and one another. The meal itself is a declaration of the compassion and mercy of God that is known in Christ, who welcomes our confession and grants us forgiveness as his sacrifice is made immediately present. The assurance of forgiveness comes before the renewal of the covenant. It is critical that we affirm that we are forgiven at this table of mercy and that we renew our covenant promises in light of this assurance, not with merely the hope that we will be forgiven. Indeed, we are forgiven specifically that we might be freed and empowered to walk in the truth. We do not live in condemnation, which is exactly why we are free, in the language of Romans 8, to walk in the Spirit.

Now we come to "nourishment" and consider how the Lord's Supper is a means by which we know the grace and strength of

God that enable us to live under the reign of Christ by the terms of the covenant. *The Book of Common Prayer* of the Anglican Church of Canada contains a wonderful section in the prayers and sayings for Holy Communion, words that reflect an ancient understanding of the meaning of this sacred event in the life of God's people. The saying that corresponds to the bread reads, "The Body of our Lord Jesus Christ, which was given for thee, preserve thy body and soul unto everlasting life: Take and eat this in remembrance that Christ died for thee, and feed on him in thy heart by faith with thanksgiving."[1] In particular, the line "feed on him in thy heart" so aptly captures a vital and profound aspect of what we experience when we come to the Lord's Supper.

The Lord's Supper is an act of worship whereby the community of faith gathered in the name of Jesus participates in a symbolic meal in which we encounter Christ afresh. It is an experience in which we find spiritual nourishment. Thus, it is with good reason that the evangelical Protestant tradition calls it a "supper." It is a liturgical and spiritual meal.

There is, though, a certain irony when it comes to the nomenclature used for this meal. Roman Catholics speak of the Eucharist, Anglicans often call it Holy Communion, and most Protestants call it the Lord's Supper. Yet it is interesting that most evangelical Protestants are a bit uncomfortable with the idea that this is actually a meal. The idea that we "feed on Christ in our hearts" is overlooked in most evangelical contexts.

But this perspective on the holy table is very much a part of the evangelical spiritual heritage, as it is of the entire Christian spiritual heritage. In the *Institutes*, the sixteenth-century Reformer John Calvin states, "The signs are bread and wine, which represent the invisible food which we receive from the body and blood of Christ . . . by which he may sustain and preserve us in the life to which he has begotten us by his word." Then later he writes, "Christ wished to testify by an external symbol that his flesh was food."[2]

---

1. The Anglican Church of Canada, *The Book of Common Prayer* (Toronto: Anglican Book Centre, 1962), 84.
2. John Calvin, *Institutes of the Christian Religion*, trans. Henry Beveridge (Grand Rapids: Eerdmans, 1979), IV, XVII, 1 (p. 557), IV, XVII, 14 (p. 567).

Through Calvin's influence, this perspective on the Lord's Supper has become an integral dimension of the Reformed understanding of this meal. The Heidelberg Catechism, for example, under the section for the Lord's Supper, reads:

> Christ has commanded me and all believers to eat this broken bread and drink this cup. . . . As surely as I receive from the hand of the one who serves, and taste with my mouth the bread and cup of the Lord, given me as sure signs of Christ's body and blood, so surely he nourishes and refreshes my soul for eternal life with his crucified body and poured-out blood.[3]

But this is also an emphasis on the Wesleyan side of the evangelical spiritual heritage. It is the idea of the Lord's Supper as nourishment (along with the fact that Christ commands that it be practiced regularly) that motivates one of John Wesley's sermons, "The Duty of Constant Communion." His insistence is that weekly (and he would even stress the value of a more frequent celebration) communion fulfills the expectation of Christ but also enables the Lord's Supper to be spiritual nourishment. He writes of this spiritual meal:

> This is food for our souls: this gives strength to perform our duty, and leads us on to perfection. If therefore we have any regard for the plain command of Christ, if we desire pardon of our sins, and if we wish for strength to believe, to love and obey God, then we should neglect no opportunity of receiving the Lord's Supper. Then we must never turn our backs on the feast which the Lord has prepared for us. We must neglect no occasion which the good providence of God affords us for this purpose.[4]

He writes acknowledging that the Church of England, of which he was a part, required participation in the Lord's Supper a minimum of three times a year (one of which was on Easter).

3. Q&A 75, "The Lord's Supper," Heidelberg Catechism, part 2, *Psalter Hymnal* (Grand Rapids: Board of Publications of the Christian Reformed Church, 1976), 36.

4. John Wesley, "The Duty of Constant Communion," in *The Works of John Wesley*, vol. 3, ed. Albert C. Outler (Nashville: Abingdon, 1986), 429.

Something that is not always recognized is the profound influence of the *devotio moderna* on the spiritual theology of the Protestant Reformation and later on the thought and practice of Wesley. *The Imitation of Christ,* attributed to Thomas à Kempis (1380–1471), is likely the most widely read devotional book in the history of the church; it epitomizes the vision and influence of this fifteenth-century movement. One of the four parts of this spiritual classic is devoted to "the blessed sacrament," evidence of the vital place of the Lord's Supper in the spirituality of the *devotio moderna.* Notable in the *Imitation* is the emphasis on Christ as the host who gives himself as spiritual food. The book speaks of Christ as the one who gives his body and his blood as the food that sustains the spiritual life, the very food and drink without which it is not possible to be a Christian. Through the "blessed sacrament," our faith is confirmed, our hope is strengthened, and our love is kindled and augmented.[5]

Both Calvin and Wesley would follow à Kempis in assuming that John 6 makes explicit reference to the Lord's Supper. But not all Christians are convinced of this. For those who are somewhat antisacramental, or at least ambivalent about the efficacy of the sacraments, it is generally unacceptable to suggest that this text has anything to do with the Lord's Supper. They are inclined to insist that this is not the point of the text at all, even though the language of eating and drinking is so prominent in the words of Jesus.

Consider the text of John 6 afresh, especially if your own tradition questions this connection. The language of this chapter in John's Gospel is an echo of the words found in both Exodus 16:15 and Psalm 78:24. In these verses, Jesus addresses two central questions: First, who is Jesus Christ? (Jesus identifies who he is.) Second, what does it mean to have faith in him? Specifically, how does this faith grow and deepen?

Who is Jesus Christ? The language is unequivocal: Jesus identifies himself with the "bread from heaven." He is the living bread, the bread of life. In so saying, he affirms *both* that he comes

---

5. Thomas à Kempis, *The Imitation of Christ,* trans. George F. Maine (London: Collins, 1957), 4/4 (p. 245). One notes in reading part 4 of the *Imitation* that the theme of "spiritual nourishment" is a constant thread in à Kempis's dialogue between Christ and the Christian (see particularly chaps. 4, 8, and 9).

from the Father and that in and through him there is life. He is life. Because he is life, we must recognize that our lives are not self-sustaining. Human life is sustained and renewed by Christ himself. How? By a response of faith. We know Jesus Christ as the living bread by believing in him, having faith in him. As Jesus states explicitly in John 6:35, "I am the bread of life. Whoever comes to me will never be hungry, and whoever believes in me will never be thirsty."

Jesus' response caused scandal: He claimed to be the living bread sent from heaven. This, of course, harkened back to the manna from heaven, which reflected the provision and mercy of God, who fed his people in the wilderness. (Jesus quotes Deuteronomy 8:3 in his response to the first temptation, as we see in Matthew 4:4.) Even though he caused offense to the religious leaders who first heard him speak these words, most contemporary readers, especially if they are Christians, are happy to accept this at face value. So far, so good. We accept that Jesus is who he says he is. It is all kept relatively cerebral and intellectual; it is something we do in our minds, in our understanding.

However, if this first statement of Jesus (that he is the bread of heaven) caused offense to his original hearers, he did not make things any better with his follow-up statement: That he gives his flesh for the life of the world (v. 51). He gives himself, his very life, for the world, for us, to sustain us and to enable us to know life in him. In saying this, Jesus raised questions not only from the religious leaders but also from his own followers, who wondered, "Who can accept this?" Who can accept the idea of eating Jesus' flesh and drinking his blood? For us "moderns," it is, of course, no less disconcerting.

But as much as we are able, we need to get beyond our squeamishness and perhaps even our shock and seek to understand this. The best way to appreciate the power of Christ's words is to highlight the unique interplay between sacrament and Word, on the one hand, and sacrament and Spirit, on the other.

We come to the table as those who have already heard the preached Word. The preaching of the Word is not incidently placed prior to the table but intentionally so. The ministry of the Word, the Old Testament and the New Testament readings, followed by the sermon, informs and gives meaning to our celebration of the Lord's Table. At the Lord's Supper, we "feed," we participate, as those whose hearts and minds have been informed and reformed by Scripture. But then, also, we come to this table with hearts lifted up and receptive once more to the Spirit of Christ. The risen Christ meets us and dwells among us and does so by his Spirit.

This second link is an important one in the theology and ministry of A. B. Simpson, the founder of the Christian and Missionary Alliance. Simpson taught of the power of Christ's real presence in the life and witness of the church in the Lord's Supper. He affirmed that while we might speak of the supper as Eucharist (joyous thanksgiving) or communion, it is rightly called the Lord's Supper because we do not merely "commune" with Christ; Christ *communicates* his grace to us in the elements. In other words, the Lord's Supper is an apt term because, as he puts it, "This expression denotes spiritual nourishment and heavenly sustenance."[6]

But Simpson goes further. He links this spiritual nourishment specifically to the ministry of the Spirit.

> In speaking of the Lord's Supper (1 Cor. 11:29) the apostle blamed them for "not discerning the Lord's body." Roman Catholics teach that in the Lord's Supper the bread and wine are converted into the actual flesh of Christ. But this is the shadow of truth; namely, that in the Lord's Supper the physical life of Jesus Christ is imparted to us as well as his spiritual blessing. It would do us no good if we could actually eat the flesh of Christ; it would be profane cannibalism. But if we can receive that which lies back of His flesh, His vital strength into our being, that is all we need. And that is the real substance of the resurrection body. He is the embodiment of life and power, and by the Holy Ghost He imparts to us that life and power as we worthily receive the sacrament and discern Him in it.[7]

Part of what I appreciate in these words is that Simpson does not fall into the trap of overreacting to a view of the Lord's Supper with which he may not fully agree. Christians typically differ

6. A. B. Simpson, *The Apostolic Church* (New York: Christian Alliance Publishing, 1898), 128.

7. A. B. Simpson, *Lord for the Body*, Tracts for the Times: Divine Healing Series (New York: Christian Alliance Publishing, c. 1900), 5.

with one another in a manner that undercuts their capacity to see the truth that exists in the perspectives of those with whom they differ. But what is most noteworthy here is that Simpson emphasizes that precisely because the Lord's Supper is a symbol, we "discern" Christ in the symbol and we know the grace of his resurrection body when we eat and drink of the bread and the cup. We know this grace through the ministry of the Spirit.

This highlights a fundamental theological and thus spiritual principle: The work of the Holy Spirit is not vague, abstract, or ethereal. The work of the Spirit, the fruit of the Spirit, finds expression in our daily lives, in the concrete, the ordinary, the mundane. So it should come as no surprise that we know the grace of the Spirit through something that is common and ordinary, something that we can touch, elements that we can actually eat. The bread and cup represent for us the spiritual food we know and have through the Word and the Spirit. These elements portray the deep longing we have for the bread from heaven, Christ himself, who by his Spirit satisfies the deepest longing of our souls. All of this comes in response to the longing of the people of God. The Welsh hymn "Guide Me, O Thou Great Jehovah" poignantly captures the human dilemma, need, and longing:

> Guide me, O Thou great Jehovah,
>   Pilgrim through this barren land;
> I am weak, but Thou art mighty,
>   Hold me with Thy powerful hand;
> Bread of heaven, Bread of heaven,
>   Feed me till I want no more;
>   Feed me till I want no more.

The force of this yearning in the human soul is not pathological but a sign of health. The church has always recognized that the great danger in the spiritual life—in life!—is that we seek satisfaction for our souls in something other than God. What Scripture attests to again and again is that only God can satisfy the deepest longings of our lives. We declare this not only in word but also in deed by the reception we give to the ministry of the Word and then, second, by our express desire to lift up our hearts and by faith feed upon Christ again. We take physical bread and an actual cup, and we partake even as we pray the prayer, "Bread of heaven, Bread of heaven, feed me till I want no more."

In the Lord's Supper, we are brought back to this central dynamic of our lives as Christian believers. In Christ, we find the bread of heaven. By faith, we meet Christ in the Word and in the table, and through his Spirit we are fed, nourished, and sustained. Thereby we declare together and to one another, but also to our common Lord, that he is the one for whom we long and that (in the words of St. Augustine) our restless souls find rest only when they find rest in him.

What sustains the human soul is Christ Jesus, his body, his blood, his very life. While Word and Spirit mediate the life of Christ to us, in the end, it is Christ himself who is the focus of our attention as we celebrate this event.

Just a small piece of bread and a sip from a cup—they seem such insignificant acts. But for the Christian community, this is a holy meal and a holy table. Christ is present, hosting the meal, and wonder of wonders, in this encounter and in this meal Christ gives himself as holy food. Therefore, it is appropriate that at this table we say, "Take and eat this in remembrance that Christ died for thee, and feed on him in thy heart by faith with thanksgiving." How often should we do so? A fitting response, perhaps, is that found in the *Introduction to the Devout Life*, where Francis de Sales insists that we should participate often in the Eucharist and indeed makes an extraordinary claim. He writes of the sacrament that "therefore whoever turns to it frequently and devoutly so effectively builds up his soul's health that it is almost impossible for him to be poisoned by evil affection of any kind."[8] It may seem like an extraordinary claim, but we need to appreciate that it is founded on the conviction that in this eating and drinking there is immediate appropriation of the grace of the ascended Lord Jesus Christ. De Sales concludes, "Those who do not have many worldly affairs" should participate often because they have the time to do so. "Those who have great undertakings" should be at the Eucharist often because they so urgently need it![9] This is, in other words, the spiritual food and

8. St. Francis de Sales, *Introduction to the Devout Life*, trans. John K. Ryan (New York: Doubleday, 1950), 104.
9. Ibid., 108.

drink of the people of God, and they need to participate often and regularly. It is appropriate to speak of the elements as "the gifts of God for the people of God." But like the manna in the desert, they are transient gifts to be received now as a gift for this day. They cannot be hoarded or guarded or saved up. What we receive is the grace of God for this day.[10]

10. This recognition that the "gifts" are *transient* was suggested to me by Leanne Van Dyk in "Reformed Sacramental Theology" (a paper given at the American Academy of Religion, November 24, 2002, Toronto).

8

ANTICIPATION

The Lord's Supper as a Declaration of Hope

When the hour came, he took his place at the table, and the apostles with him. He said to them, "I have eagerly desired to eat this Passover with you before I suffer; for I tell you, I will not eat it until it is fulfilled in the kingdom of God." Then he took a cup, and after giving thanks he said, "Take this and divide it among yourselves; for I tell you that from now on I will not drink of the fruit of the vine until the kingdom of God comes." Then he took a loaf of bread, and when he had given thanks, he broke it and gave it to them, saying, "This is my body, which is given for you. Do this in remembrance of me." And he did the same with the cup after supper, saying, "This cup that is poured out for you is the new covenant in my blood. But see, the one who betrays me is with me, and his hand is on the table. For the Son of Man is going as it has been determined, but woe to that one by whom he is betrayed!" Then they began to ask one another, which one of them it could be who would do this.

A dispute also arose among them as to which one of them was to be regarded as the greatest. But he said to them, "The kings of the Gentiles lord it over them; and those in authority over them are called benefactors. But not so with you; rather the greatest among you must become like the youngest, and the leader like

one who serves. For who is greater, the one who is at the table
or the one who serves? Is it not the one at the table? But I am
among you as one who serves."

Luke 22:14–27

An intriguing line written by William Sloan Coffin reads, "The
Eucharist quenches my thirst for hope."[1] This chapter probes
what it means to speak in this way about this sacred meal. We
will consider how the Lord's Supper is a means by which hope
is both declared and cultivated.

We live and work in a discouraging world, and our capacity to make a difference for good—whether at home or in our
occupations, in the church, or in the world—resides in large
measure in whether we do what we are called to do out of an
abiding confidence that one day all will be well. We need to be
a people of hope.

An authentic hope is one that sees reality clearly. To live in
hope demands a realism about our world—that we see the world
the way it is. What hope gives us is the capacity to recognize
that what we see is not the last word. Living with hope, then, allows us to see our circumstances clearly, recognize the presence
and power of all that is wrong, and not sentimentalize or—and
this distinction is crucial—overly dramatize all that we think is
wrong. In other words, the genius of living with hope is that we
are able to describe reality without downplaying the wrong or,
conversely, having to be fearmongers. Hope enables us both to
see and to act truthfully.

The hope of the church is intimately linked with the longing
of creation. We are reminded in the Epistle to the Romans that
the entire creation waits in eager longing for the resolution that
comes with the consummation of the kingdom (Rom. 8:19) and
that this hope will not disappoint us (Rom. 5:5).

We long, then, for hope; it is the only way we can live. Part of
the marvel of the Lord's Supper is that, in the words of William
Sloan Coffin, it "quenches our thirst for hope." By this act we
are proclaiming together that our hope is in Christ, and in this

1. William Sloan Coffin, *Credo: The Wisdom of an American Prophet* (Louisville:
Westminster John Knox, 2004), 140.

act, our hope is renewed as again we are enabled to live in a discouraging world as a people of hope. The Lord's Supper is a meal of *anticipation*.

Two Meals

This anticipation is evident in each of the references to the Lord's Supper but particularly in the Gospel of Luke (chap. 22). This comes as no surprise if we recall that Luke is the Gospel that is most intentionally and deeply historical. The Gospel writer brings a historical consciousness to the accounts of Jesus' ministry and teaching; he is precise about past events as he looks ahead to future events.

What captures our attention in this account of the Last Supper is that Jesus is seeking to impress on the hearts and minds of his disciples the reality that this meal foreshadows another meal. Jesus reveals to his disciples that while they partake of this meal, there is another meal that he anticipates. In verses 15 and 16, we read that Jesus has eagerly desired to eat this meal. Why? Because he knows that he will not eat of it again until the kingdom that is yet to come. Then in verse 18 he refers to drinking of the fruit of the vine again in the kingdom—looking ahead to the consummation of the kingdom, which he emphasizes in verses 19–20. Then while speaking of their lives in this world and of his own trials in verse 28, he stresses the point yet again as he looks ahead to the coming of a kingdom in which they will eat and drink at Jesus' table (vv. 29–30). Thus, we have two meals in our sight. While eating one meal, Jesus is looking ahead to another.

The hope of the church and the world is symbolized and realized by a meal—the marriage supper of the Lamb (Rev. 19), a glorious feast hosted by Jesus himself. The Lord's Supper anticipates this meal and is a foretaste of the joy and the sense of well-being that is represented by that heavenly banquet (see Luke 22:30; Rev. 19:7, 9; 21:2, 9; 22:17).

In 1 Corinthians, we read that as we eat and drink, we "proclaim the Lord's death until he comes" (11:26). Thus, it follows, as Geoffrey Wainwright puts it, that the Eucharist is celebrated in the time of *hope* before the second coming of Christ, of which the first coming of Christ was a *promise*. The church recalls before the Father in thanksgiving the first coming of Christ and prays for the second coming of Christ in final fulfilment of that promise."[2] Or as C. H. Dodd puts it, in the Eucharist, we not only look back and remember but also look forward: "We are at the moment of His coming, with angels and arch-angels and the company of heaven, in the twinkling of an eye at the last trump."[3]

It is the act of eating together that locates us in the events that are yet to come. Eating is an important motif in the Gospel of Luke. The Gospel writer describes ten meals, and some parables in Luke also involve eating and drinking. Consistently, in Luke, a meal symbolizes not only the blessing of God but also, in particular, the eschatological blessing, the arrival of the kingdom. Whether it is the feast following the lost son's return or the Last Supper, there is an air of expectation, of looking forward to what is yet to be.

The Last Supper is a farewell, no doubt. But it is not the last word. It is a meal that points to another meal. The two meals are intentionally linked. Each time we celebrate this special meal in the context of our worship, we look ahead and identify with the heavenly banquet, a meal that will be celebrated on that day when all things are made right. We declare in our participation, in our eating and drinking, that evil, wrong, and pain do not have the last word and that we live now with an eager anticipation of the future. The celebration of the Lord's Supper anticipates another meal and prepares us for it. We eat together, yearning together for another day; we eat knowing it is coming. We are eager for Christ Jesus to usher in his kingdom.

But just as this meal, the Lord's Supper, anticipates the other meal, it is also the case that the heavenly banquet, the marriage supper of the Lamb, permeates this meal. The Lord's Supper is infused with hope; our present is shaped, informed, and ultimately transformed by the reality of a meal that is yet to come. In this holy meal, in the here and now, we do not have only an opportunity for eager anticipation of what is yet to come. In this

2. Geoffrey Wainwright, *Eucharist and Eschatology* (New York: Oxford University Press, 1981).

3. C. H. Dodd, *The Apostolic Preaching and Its Developments* (London: Hodder & Stoughton, 1936), 114–15.

meal, that future event is present. Our present is invaded and infused by the future. The gospel arrives on our doorstep, and we are enabled to live with hope in a discouraging world.

The Anglican tradition so effectively highlights that the Lord's Supper is an act of spiritual nourishment in which we feed on Christ by faith. The Eastern Orthodox tradition effectively demonstrates that this meal is an act of renewed hope. Alexander Schmemann, for example, emphasizes this when he stresses that the Lord's Supper is an event in space and time, in *this* space and time, in the here and now, in the uncertainties and discouragement of this time.[4] In other words, the Lord's Supper is not an escape from our time or place. We do not sentimentalize our world, turn our backs on our world, or forget about our world. On the contrary, this event is very much one in which we participate as those who are unavoidably in this world. However, as Schmemann notes, we enter into this meal and participate symbolically in what we hope for, the future renewal of the creation. We can live now, truly live in this broken world, because we have hope. We see this world through the lens of God's prophetic Word.

The Lord's Supper cuts the cord of cynicism and defeatism that so easily binds our hearts and minds and leaves us defeated. Through the celebration of this holy meal, we enter again into a deep and confident awareness that Christ is on the throne of the universe and that we can rest on his faithfulness.

The Signs of Hope

We urgently need people of hope in government and in education as teachers and administrators. We need people of hope in our neighborhoods whose quiet confidence in God enables everyone around them to live with joy in a broken world. In business, in the arts, in work with the elderly and children, we make a difference only when we are people of hope.

If the Lord's Supper is the renewal of this hope, if this is the event in which we are encouraged, it is appropriate to ask, Well, then, what is the evidence of this? If we are people of hope,

4. Alexander Schmemann, *For the Life of the World: Sacraments and Orthodoxy* (Crestwood, NY: St. Vladimir's Press, 1973), 139.

how do we know this? What are the indicators that through the grace we receive in the Lord's Supper our courage is being renewed?[5]

There are two defining signs of hope, indicators that we are being encouraged. The first is joy. Anticipation fosters a steady and abiding joy and assurance in those who participate in the Lord's Supper.

One of the unfortunate side effects of treating the Lord's Supper as a mere memorial is that this aspect is often lacking: the joyful anticipation, the celebration of the reign of Christ in the world. It should be manifestly clear that when we celebrate this holy meal, we drink together of the cup of joy. The key to this joy is our confidence, our faith, that Christ is now on the throne and that one day this will be apparent to all. At the revelation of this wonder, all things will be made right, and justice and peace will embrace. We are no longer cynics, for this joy permeates every dimension of our lives, our relationships, and our work.

It begins, of course, in the meal itself. For many Protestants, the memorial motif means that we are specifically remembering the death of Christ (and seeking to relive the Last Supper and the sense of doom that darkness is coming over the earth). It feels like a funeral service. But contrast this with the early church, for whom the Lord's Supper marked not only the death of Christ but also his resurrection. It thus highlighted their confidence that one day Jesus would make all things right: "Day by day, as they spent much time together in the temple, they broke bread at home and ate their food with glad and generous hearts, praising God and having the goodwill of all the people" (Acts 2:46–47).

But there is more. There is a necessary second indicator that we are people of hope: generous, active, sacrificial service. If our joy is not matched by concrete action in the world, if our renewed hope does not infuse our lives with both joy and engagement, then something is amiss, for the Lord's Supper is not an escape or an act by which we look to the future because we have given up on the present. Just the opposite. We are enabled to live with joy in the present, and we are enabled to make a difference in the present. This is the fruit of hope.

---

5. By implication, this gives us the terms of reference for knowing when we are discouraged.

We eat together as an act of faith, confident that one day the reign of Christ will be complete. We eat looking forward to that day. But we also eat having prayed the prayer, "Thy will be done on earth as it is in heaven." In other words, we eat longing for the future meal but also desiring and resolving to live *now* in light of the consummation of the kingdom. This means that the Lord's Supper nurtures our apostolic vision for life in the present, enabling us to engage our lives now not as cynics but as men and women of hope. We move from this meal back to the world eager to live a life consistent with the hope we have in the gospel.

As such, the Lord's Supper has a profound missionary significance: It is a sign (and a proclamation) of the great feast toward which all history is moving, the day on which every knee will bow and every person will proclaim Christ as Lord (Phil. 2). We know that one day all will be well, and so we are renewed in our resolve that in word and deed we will witness now, in our lives, our relationships, our work—both in the church and the world—to the reign of Christ. Our hope is for all humanity, for each society and city, and indeed for the entire creation. If we live and work with a concern for the environment, it is because we have hope. In the Lord's Supper, we declare that no situation is inherently hopeless, and as a result, we reenter the world encouraged to give time, energy, and talent to making a difference for good.

But our way of being in the world has a particular mark or stance. This is emphasized by an extraordinary exchange Jesus has with his disciples on the occasion of the Last Supper. Jesus is celebrating the Passover with his disciples, and he does so with a heavy heart, for he knows that he is going to the cross and that one of them will betray him. Then in the midst of this, there is a debate. We read, "A dispute also arose among them as to which one of them was to be regarded as the greatest" (Luke 22:24). We might be surprised that this topic would come up, except for the fact that Jesus is talking about the kingdom and about his reign in this world and its consummation at the last day. They are, after all, talking about a kingdom, and so, naturally, matters of authority and who has authority and what is important and who is great tend to come to the fore. Jesus responds very specifically to the dispute by putting everything in perspective when he says, "I am among you as one who serves" (v. 27). As we know from this text and others, greatness in the kingdom is found through service.

Jesus then goes on in the next verse to look ahead to the eating and drinking that is yet to come in the kingdom. But what he has established is this: On *this* day, while we live with anticipation, while we look to *that* day, while we live now as people of hope, we are those who serve.

Many know from personal experience that when we lack hope, we lose the motivation to serve, to be patient with others, to give and to give generously. We start to compare ourselves to one another and complain if we do not think we are being treated well; we calculate. When we are encouraged, we are more likely to serve with a willing spirit, to take on the ordinary tasks, the mundane tasks, to (as Jesus says) "wait on tables," and to do so with joy and humility. This is what it means, at least in part, to live in hope—to be generous and eager servants.

When we celebrate the Lord's Supper, the ascended Lord Jesus Christ himself is in our midst as one who will ultimately host us at the marriage supper of the Lamb. We believe in the "real presence," one might say. But as Jesus himself stresses, he is among us as one who serves. This is the wonder of this table. Jesus meets us and hosts a meal; he forgives us and feeds us. Through intimate communion and fellowship with him and with our sisters and brothers, we look back (in remembrance), but we also look ahead to the kingdom that is yet to come. We renew our baptismal identity and vows as people of the new covenant. And with hope we identify with the Lord himself, who is the servant of all.

9

EUCHARIST

The Lord's Supper as a Joyous Thanksgiving Celebration

Day by day, as they spent much time together in the temple, they broke bread at home and ate their food with glad and generous hearts, praising God and having the goodwill of all the people.

Acts 2:46–47

The Lord's Supper is Eucharist—the seventh and final word to be considered—a word that indicates an intimate link between joy, thanksgiving, and the grace of God.[1]

The Priority of Joy

One of the remarkable persons of the twentieth century is the English author G. K. Chesterton, an essayist, a writer of detective fiction, an apologist for the Christian faith. He suggests, at

---

1. In Greek, the connection is more obvious; the words *joy*, *grace*, and *thanksgiving* all have the same root.

the conclusion of one of his most important works, titled *Orthodoxy*, that it is in the very character of a human life to have joy, that it is *native* to us, to use his word. He points out that for most people, if they are happy, they are happy about little things "but sad about the big ones."[2] But this is not the way it is supposed to be. Indeed, he contends that we are most human, most ourselves, most who we were created to be, when joy is the fundamental thing about us. If we have grief, and we will, it is necessarily on the surface. It is a passing, transient emotion. If we are discouraged, it is only like a brief holiday (he calls it a "half holiday"). But, Chesterton insists, the fundamental stuff of who we are and the way we live is that we are marked by a deep and "expansive" joy. It is this that drew him to the Christian faith, for he saw, as he himself would insist throughout his entire life, that Christianity is first and foremost a religion of joy.

This is congruent with the words of the New Testament, evident most, perhaps, in the words of Jesus, who declares to his disciples that he has come that their joy may be made complete (John 15:11; 17:13). While this is certainly not all there is to being a Christian, Chesterton is on to something basic to our Christian identity. It is confirmed over and over again throughout the church's history: Joy is not an optional extra, a nice little touch in the Christian life that may or may not actually be present. It is, rather, the deciding factor. The presence of joy is the definitive evidence that we are Christians, that we live as those who believe in the resurrection of Jesus Christ.

However, this does not mean that we are always happy. We believe in the resurrection, but the full impact and the effects of the resurrection are still to come. For now we wait, and while we see signs and indicators of hope, we still live in a fallen and broken world. If we have joy now, it is because of faith, not sight; it is because we believe that Jesus, even today, is the ascended Lord who sits on the throne of the universe.

Integrity demands that we feel the force of the brokenness of this world—anger at injustice, discouragement in the face of setback, mourning when there is loss, fear when our lives are

---

2. G. K. Chesterton, *Orthodoxy* (New York: John Lane Company, 1909), 296. It is interesting to observe that Chesterton wrote *Orthodoxy* while he was *becoming* a Christian.

threatened. But we cannot stay there; we cannot (as I once heard it put) camp there. Emotionally, this is not our true home. We are most ourselves when we live in joy, for which we were created. This is what marked the life of the early church—a deep and expansive joy. Therefore, though we are angry, we do not let the sun go down on our anger; we do not stay there. Though we are discouraged, we are not cynics but respond eagerly and allow God to renew our hope. Though we are afraid, we cast our cares on him and receive the peace that transcends all understanding (Phil. 4:7). This is because, ultimately, we believe that Christ is the ascended Lord, and we believe that this is the most fundamental fact of the universe.

It is important to highlight this link with the resurrection. The early Christian church was a community of joy; a deep gladness marked their common life (Acts 2:42–47). Even in the midst of persecution they were a people of joy. Christians throughout the centuries have valued the account of Paul and Silas imprisoned (Acts 16). In that horrid place, where they were flogged and their feet were fastened in stocks, in the middle of the night they are praying and singing hymns. Clearly, their joy was a fundamental characteristic that informed and gave credibility to their witness to their fellow prisoners and to the Philippian jailer, whose response is well known: He and his family came to faith in Christ.

Joy and the Lord's Supper

In Luke 24, the Gospel writer speaks of the experience of the disciples, who after the resurrection recognized Jesus in *the breaking of the bread* (vv. 30–31). Luke is clearly speaking of the Lord's Supper, and with this phrase he is intentionally highlighting the link between this meal and the resurrection, or better, the link between this meal and the presence of the risen Christ in the midst of God's people.

Then Luke picks up on this motif in Acts 2:42, where he observes that those who responded to the preaching of Peter on the day of Pentecost devoted themselves to the apostles' teaching, the breaking of bread, and prayer. Then in the verses that follow, he stresses that they broke bread in houses—their places of worship—with glad and generous hearts. It is no wonder that this was the case, for in the breaking of bread, they were celebrating the resurrection and the ascension and thus the actual, dynamic presence of the risen Christ. In the breaking of the bread, they entered into fellowship with the ascended Christ!

When we speak of the Lord's Supper, every dimension of meaning points to the experience of joy. When we speak of the Lord's Supper as a remembrance, we are not remembering a dead Christ. Rather, an event of the past infuses our present with the gospel. Yes, we look back in remembrance, but the Lord's Supper is an event in which the past is made present. When we speak of the Lord's Supper as communion or as bread from heaven, it is because we believe that in this meal we encounter a risen Christ who meets us, draws us into fellowship with him, and nourishes us through the outpouring of his Spirit.

Therefore, it is all meaningless, hopeless, if Christ is not risen and does not sit on the throne of the universe (1 Cor. 15:19). But thanks be to God, Christ is risen and meets us, greets us by name, and draws us to himself, empowering us afresh through his Spirit. It is no wonder that they broke bread "with glad and generous hearts."

More than one spiritual tradition has effectively captured this perspective when speaking of the Lord's Supper, but it is difficult to overlook the powerful emphasis on joy in the eucharistic hymns of John and Charles Wesley. These hymns rightly affirm all the dimensions of meaning of the Lord's Supper, but it is joy in the presence of the risen and ascended Christ that arises again and again as we sing them. Consider the words of "O Glorious Instrument Divine":

> O Glorious instrument Divine
>   Which blessings to our souls conveys,
> Brings with the hallow'd bread and wine
>   His strengthening and refreshing grace,
> Presents His bleeding sacrifice,
>   His all-reviving death applies!
>
> Glory to God who reigns above,
>   But suffer'd once for man below!
> With joy we celebrate His love,
>   And thus His precious passion show,

102

Till in the clouds our Lord we see,
And shout with all His saints—Tis He![3]

Joy and Thanksgiving: The Lord's Supper as Eucharist

A recurring theme in the history of Christian spirituality is that an emphasis on joy is consistently found where the Lord's Supper is spoken of as Eucharist. The word *Eucharist* arises from the Greek word for thanksgiving or blessing. This is the sense, for example, of the words of Paul in 1 Corinthians 10, where he speaks of the cup as the cup of blessing (of Eucharist) (v. 16). To give thanks is to bless—we give thanks at a meal by saying a blessing. Thus, the apostle Paul speaks of the Lord's Supper as a Eucharist, an apt and appropriate designation for the holy meal. This is one of the most ancient ways of designating the Lord's Supper, evidenced in the *Didache*, an early church teaching document from roughly the year A.D. 100.

From early on, the church has viewed the Lord's Supper as an occasion like none other in which the community of faith gives thanks. First and foremost, the church gives thanks to the Father, the source of all good gifts. John Chrysostom, an early church father, suggests how Paul would respond if he were asked to explain what he means by the word *blessing* when he speaks of the cup of blessing in 1 Corinthians 10:16. Paul would reply, "When I say blessing, I mean thanksgiving, and when I say thanksgiving I am unfolding the whole treasure of God's goodness and calling to mind his marvelous gifts."[4]

At the Last Supper, Jesus followed traditional Jewish practice when at the beginning of the meal he pronounced a blessing and "gave thanks" over the cup. Ever since, we have recognized that

---

3. Charles Wesley, *Hymns of the Lord's Supper* (1745), no. 115, cited in J. E. Rattenbury, *The Eucharistic Hymns of John and Charles Wesley* (London: Epworth Press, 1948), 115. I thank Linda Tue for drawing my attention to this hymn. In an unpublished essay, she observes that 79 of the 166 hymns in the collection of hymns on the Lord's Supper contain either explicit or implicit references to and expressions of joy.

4. John Chrysostom, "Homilies on 1 Corinthians 24:1–2 (on 1 Cor. 10:16–17)," in *Documents in Early Christian Thought*, ed. Maurice Wiles and Mark Santer (Cambridge: Cambridge University Press, 1975), 197.

the Lord's Supper is a Eucharist; it is a thanksgiving celebration in the tradition of the ancient Jewish prayers of thanks to the Creator and Redeemer of Israel. All the words of institution, regardless of the denomination from which they come, highlight this reality. This is a Eucharist. As Jesus gave thanks, so we give thanks.

We give thanks for the providential care of God. The Eucharist, the Lord's Supper, is an event in which we declare that God is good and that his mercies endure forever. The whole created order testifies to his goodness. In the bread and the cup, we have symbols of this plenty. They represent the things of this earth, all of the gifts of God that are poured out upon us. God is so good.

In blessing the creation and giving thanks for the goodness of God in creation, we declare in the celebration of the Lord's Supper that there is hope for all creation. We give thanks as an act of hope and a rejection of despair and cynicism.

We also give thanks for the mighty deeds of God, for the gift and glory of creation but also for the gracious goodness of a God who has acted for us in Christ Jesus. In our remembering, we give thanks. God is Creator and Redeemer! We give thanks for Christ Jesus himself and for the gift of his Spirit in our lives. We thank God for his work in Christ Jesus, for the cross and the resurrection, for the amazing grace that would reach out in love and conquer sin and death. In the words of Psalm 100, we enter his gates with thanksgiving. The deep joy that we have in the experience of an encounter with the risen Christ is specifically (and intentionally) a joy that comes through thanksgiving.

All of this has found wonderful expression in the prayers that attend the celebration of the Lord's Supper. There is a discernable theme, even a recurring wording, that runs from the ancient prayers of St. Basil and St. Chrysostom through the Roman missal to the Anglican and Methodist orders of worship and other contemporary worship books. For example, the Presbyterian order of worship includes the "Great Thanksgiving," which opens with a call to thanksgiving and then turns into the thankful declaration of the goodness of God in the prayers said by the presiding minister. It reads (the first part is read responsively between the liturgist or pastor and the people):

Lift up your hearts.
  We lift them up to the Lord.
Give thanks to God, for he is good.
  His love is everlasting.
Lift up your hearts.
  We lift them up to the Lord.
Let us give thanks to the Lord our God.
  It is right to give him thanks and praise.

Holy Lord, Father almighty, everlasting God: We thank you for commanding light out of darkness, for dividing the waters into sea and dry land, for creating the whole world and calling it good. We thank you for making us in your image to live with each other in love; for the breath of life, the gift of speech, and the freedom to choose your way. You have told us your purpose in the commandments to Moses, and called for justice in the cry of the prophets. Through long generations, you have been fair and kind to all your children.[5]

The prayer continues with a celebration of the holiness of God followed by thanksgiving for the salvation that is known through Jesus Christ and, of course, the gift of the Spirit. The intent, as with all the classic prayers of thanksgiving that it echoes, is to make the Lord's Supper an act of gratitude.

Thanksgiving and Sacrifice

Consistent with the Jewish tradition, thanksgiving is offered through sacrifice. Indeed, the entire sacrificial system was a structure and form for giving thanks. Thus, there is an appropriate link in Christian thought between Eucharist and sacrifice, between thanksgiving and the act of sacrifice. The Lord's Supper is a sacrifice, an offering of praise and thanksgiving.

When we think of the Lord's Supper as a sacrifice, we are making an identification with the Old Testament sacrificial system. The New Testament texts that speak of the supper consistently include phrases and allusions to the sacrificial system, whether

5. *The Worship Book: Services and Hymns* (Philadelphia: Westminster, 1966), 34–35.

it is "the blood of the covenant" in Matthew 26:28, which comes from Exodus 24:8, or the eating of the sacrifices in 1 Corinthians 10:18, which harkens back to the peace offerings mentioned in Leviticus 7:11–18. These references link the Lord's Supper to the sacrificial system, and association is made with one of those sacrifices in particular, the peace offering. What is distinctive about the peace offering is that the participants ate in the presence of the Lord as a *joyful act of fellowship* with God. As an act of celebration of the mercy and goodness of God, the worshipers joyously ate the offering in one another's company and as an intentional act of communion with the Lord.

C. John Collins has made the valuable observation that in the early church—the years immediately after the apostles—it was common to link the Lord's Supper with the peace offering. He points out that for the early church theologians the Passover was the historical *occasion* for the Last Supper, but the Passover did not exhaust the meaning of the meal that Jesus instituted. Indeed, the peace offering, which was celebrated regularly by the Old Testament people of God, was as much a part of the meaning of the Lord's Supper as the Passover.[6] The problem with closely linking the Passover with the Lord's Supper is that it becomes easy to conclude that this is to be an annual event rather than a weekly practice of the church. Collins observes that from early in the history of the church the Lord's Supper was observed weekly, evidence again of the link with the peace offering.

The Gifts of God for the People of God

While it is surely appropriate to come to the table through confession and sober self-reflection, this is at most preliminary and "in passing" as we get to the heart of the matter, which is a joyful celebration of the goodness of God. The primary emotional contour of this event should be not grave deliberation but joyous thanksgiving. We give thanks for the providential goodness of God and for the mighty deeds of God. The ancient *Didache*

6. C. John Collins, "The Eucharist as Christian Sacrifice: How Patristic Authors Can Help Us Read the Bible," *Westminster Theological Journal* 66 (2004): 1–23.

also includes specific thanks for the assembly, for the church gathered. We thank God for one another, and we enter into our common fellowship as thankful recipients.

It is specifically as we give thanks for these gifts that the Spirit renews and sustains our joy. When we give thanks, when we celebrate the Eucharist (thanksgiving), we lift up our hearts. The very act of giving thanks brings down our guard before the Spirit of the living God, who fills our hearts, calls us, and enables us to live, from the core and depth of our beings, as people of the resurrection who live now in communion with their ascended Lord.

A simple but powerful principle of the spiritual life is that thankful people are happy people. It is not that the church does not see the brokenness of the world and the pain that intersects so much of human life. It is not that the church is naïve and does not care about this pain; the Christian community sees and feels keenly the brokenness of the world. But in the celebration of the Eucharist, the church declares that in the midst of all that is wrong, God is the ruler yet,[7] and God is good. The church believes that something bigger and more ultimate stands at the center of the mess. As Chesterton often insisted, we take joy in the deep things, those things that matter most. Yes, we grieve. But we know that those things will one day pass. When we take the larger view, when we think cosmically, the center of the universe is a throne, and on this throne sits the risen Lord Jesus Christ. This, more than anything, establishes us as people of joy.

The holy meal sustains joy in our worship but then, of course, in our *lives*—in our relationships and our work in the world. The Lord's Supper establishes a people whose fundamental disposition is joy. This is our posture of heart in coming to worship and to the celebration of the Lord's Supper, but what we find is that the celebration at this table further shapes our hearts and cultivates a capacity to live in the world as a people with an abiding joy.

Joy, gladness, and generosity, then, are indicators of the presence of the Spirit in our midst. But more, the Lord's Supper has the unique capacity to mediate the grace of the Spirit to us, to

---

7. Malthie D. Babcock, "This Is My Father's World," *Hymns of the Christian Life* (Harrisburg, PA: Christian Publications, 1978), 28.

order our affections in good times and bad, to enable us to walk by faith, to renew our covenant commitments, to delight and find great joy in communion with Christ and one another, and to live now in light of the great celebration we will have at the marriage supper of the Lamb (Rev. 19:6–9). The Lord's Supper is not an escape from a world of difficulty and drudgery; it is, rather, a joyous meal that, in turn, enables us to live in truth and joy in a fallen and broken world.

PART 3

CONCLUDING
OBSERVATIONS

10

THE PRESENCE OF CHRIST AND THE MINISTRY OF THE SPIRIT

The Form of Our Celebration

Any examination of the meaning of the Lord's Supper will, of course, raise questions about its practice: How often should it be celebrated? Who should preside? What forms of bread and beverage are appropriate and truly constitute the elements of the Lord's Supper? and so on. Concerning the elements, for example, some will insist that wheat and wine are ordained by Christ and that if these are not available in a particular country, they need to be brought in.[1] Others, in contrast, will argue that diversity is acceptable and that, in the words of John Calvin, "these things are indifferent, and left free to the Church."[2] What is clear is that even if a community uses bread and wine, this may have quite diverse expressions. The Lord's Supper is celebrated

1. Thomas Aquinas writes, "Wheat and wine are not native to every country, but the amounts needed are easily transported" (*Summa Theologiae: A Concise Translation*, ed. Timothy McDermott [Westminster, MD: Christian Classics, 1989], 570, part 74, par. 1).
2. John Calvin, *Institutes of the Christian Religion*, trans. Henry Beveridge (Grand Rapids: Eerdmans, 1979), IV, XVII, par. 21 (p. 574).

in different forms in different cultures and Christian traditions. Various denominational groups have their emphases, not just on the elements but on a host of other questions that in the end shape how this meal is observed.

This does not mean that everything or just anything constitutes the Lord's Supper. The practice matters, and thus it is fitting to ask, What constitutes theologically appropriate practice? Apart from the insistence that the observance of the Lord's Supper must accompany and, when observed, *follow* the preached Word (so that our celebration is informed and shaped by our listening to the Word and so that the symbolic actions carry the meaning given them by the Word), I will here address only three questions.

With respect to frequency, most liturgical historians conclude that for the early church, including the apostolic church, the Lord's Supper was celebrated weekly. The command of Christ implies a continuing and regular practice. Acts 20:7 suggests that the early Christian communities believed they were to celebrate the Lord's Supper each time they gathered: "on the first day of the week, when we met to break bread." Obviously, this was a gathering of worship, with a liturgy that included songs and hymns and no doubt the ministry of the Word. But it is interesting that this event is spoken of as one in which they gathered for the breaking of bread. While there is no mandate prescribing weekly observance, contemporary Christian communities are on the right track when they lean toward more frequent celebration of the holy meal, recognizing that nothing is lost and much is gained in breaking bread often.

With respect to the elements, if we are going to use bread, then it should look, taste, and feel like bread. The reason, in part, is that the incarnation was real, not an artificial humanity. When this perspective is placed alongside the obvious reference to a *single* loaf in 2 Corinthians 10:17, it would seem that even if diced bread or some other form of bread, such as cracker chips, is necessary for ease of distribution, particularly in large assemblies, at the very least an actual loaf—something that *looks* like bread—should be used for the words of institution.[3] A single

---

3. Ideally, a nourishing, whole-grain bread, not a nonnutritive confection. Rosemary Haughton suggests that the sacrament must use ordinary bread, not unlike-bread bread.

loaf of bread is in itself a declaration of our common identity as a people. We are one.

Third, the question of who presides is an important one. Here, too, there will be diversity of practice and opinion regarding what is appropriate. My own conclusion is that this is the Lord's Supper, but it is also the supper of the church. This means that the one who presides does so in the name of Christ but also on behalf of the church. Therefore, it is fitting that the person who presides is designated by the church, either through ordination or some other formal act, so that he or she acts not in his or her own authority but as the representative of the community.

In the end, however, three values or ideals provide the contours of our practice. First, the Lord's Supper needs to be a meal of hopeful thanksgiving. Second, it must become an occasion to celebrate and experience the love of God. Third, it must enable us to be a community of disciples who choose to live together under the reign of Christ. Within this framework, there is plenty of room for diversity of practice. In the end, however, it is best to remember that this is a *simple* event—an encounter between the people of God and the Lord of the church.

The Presence of Christ

The Lord's Supper *is* a simple event. The people of God eat and drink together, usually amounts of bread and wine that are so small as to seem insignificant. But again and again they gather, and in this simple act they portray something whose meaning is vast. Surely it is this vast dimension of meaning that led St. Francis de Sales to speak of it as "the sun of all spiritual exercises."[4] The significance and experience of this event are polyphonic—multiple meanings, voices, and perspectives coming together in one event. Indeed, something is lost when only one dimension of meaning is experienced or taught within a Christian community.

But though it is an event of multiple meanings, the Lord's Supper remains a simple event: It is an encounter with Christ

---

4. St. Francis de Sales, *Introduction to the Devout Life,* trans. John K. Ryan (New York: Doubleday, 1950), 92.

Jesus. As the people of God gather, the invitation to come and receive the elements is ultimately an invitation to meet Christ, to commune with Christ, and to identify with Christ—to know, love, and obey. Just as baptism is an act of union with Christ in his death and resurrection, so the Lord's Supper is the central event in which the community of faith identifies with that which more than anything else defines its life. Therefore, though it is a simple act, because it is an act of encounter with Christ, it is an event that sustains the human soul. The poem of George Herbert captures it well:

> Having rais'd me to look up,
> In a cup
> Sweetly he doth meet my taste.
> But I still being low and short,
> Farre from court,
> Wine becomes a wing at last.
>
> For with it alone I flie,
> To the skie
> Where I wipe mine eyes, and see
> What I seek, for what I sue;
> Him I view,
> What hath done so much for me.[5]

Here at this meal our hearts take wing; here is food for the soul, comfort for the disheartened, strength for the weary. Why? Because it is an event in which we meet Jesus.

But how? How is Christ present at or in the celebration of the Lord's Supper? For some traditions, the presence of Christ is found in the elements themselves.[6] All attention is given to the bread and the wine as being, as much as can be expressed in human language, the body and blood of the Lord Jesus Christ.

5. George Herbert (d. 1633), "The Banquet," lines 37–38, in *The English Poems of George Herbert*, ed. C. A. Patrides (London: Rowman & Littlefield, 1974), 186.

6. I am indebted to Wolfhart Pannenberg for this summary of diverse views on the presence of Christ in the Lord's Supper (Wolfhart Pannenberg, *Systematic Theology*, vol. 3, trans. Geoffrey W. Bromiley [Grand Rapids: Eerdmans, 1998], 302–5). I follow Pannenberg in the conclusion that the genius of the event is the dynamic presence of the ascended Christ, who is known and experienced through the ministry of the Spirit.

For other traditions, the presence of Christ is found not in the elements but in the gathered community. The people make up the body of Christ. The people, in their gathering, make Christ present. This view rightly affirms that the sacrament is not only the *Lord's* Supper; it is also the supper of the *church.* In their extreme forms, these two views almost discount each other. In the first, the Eucharist can be celebrated alone by a priest, with no one else present. In the second, the elements themselves seem almost incidental—only "tokens" at best.[7]

A third view suggests that the presence of Christ is found in the actions of the community—the specific act of eating and drinking. Though the Lutheran tradition does not limit the presence of Christ to the act of consumption, on the whole, the Reformers—Luther and Calvin—would agree that the promise of Christ is linked with the *use* of the elements.

All three of these views capture something important. The elements matter; there is little doubt that when Jesus said, "This is my body" he was making explicit reference to the bread he held in his hand. Symbols matter and must be taken seriously.[8] Similarly, this is an act of a gathered community, so much so that the Lord's Supper makes no sense apart from the people who together eat and drink in response to the invitation of Christ. Further, the eating and drinking are in some respects the heart of the event. The elements mean nothing in themselves, and the people gathered together do not constitute the Lord's Supper. It is the gathered community who then *eat and drink* together. Thus, all three perspectives are integral and necessary as we speak of the presence of Christ in this holy meal. However, our focus is not, in the end, on the elements, the people around us, our drinking and eating, or the diverse meanings that we rightly associate with this occasion. The focus is on the one who hosts the meal, Christ Jesus. In our words of institution and in

7. For some groups, notably in the believers' church tradition, the words "This is my body" refer not to the bread or to the elements but to the community of disciples.

8. This merits a theological caution: The symbol matters, but it is not to be confused with what is symbolized. We can and must affirm the rightful place of symbols—to honor the symbol is to honor that to which the symbol points. However, the symbol is a symbol, and we should not make of the symbol what belongs in the end to Christ alone.

our acts of remembrance, self-examination, and thanksgiving, we are but entering into the work of Christ. And so, ultimately, what carries the day—the energy that makes this meal a means by which our deepest longings are fulfilled—is that the Lord's Supper is the *Lord's*.

The Ministry of the Spirit

We appreciate this most when we affirm that the Lord's Supper is a gift from God. We speak of the "gifts of God for the people of God" and thus with joy receive the elements that are offered. But in so doing, we are consciously and intentionally receiving *the* gift from God, the person of the Lord Jesus Christ. Christ, then, is not a thing but a personal, engaging presence who meets us and gives himself to us. But he does so specifically through this event when our celebration is informed by the *Word* of God and infused by the *Spirit* of God.

On the one hand, this conviction finds expression in the order of our worship; the Lord's Supper appropriately follows the ministry of the Word—the oral reading and the exposition of Scripture. We listen and we eat, and our eating is the act of those who have listened and received the Word.

But it is vital that we also appreciate that we know the presence of Christ through the grace-filled actions of the Spirit. It is not the elements or the community that effect the presence of Christ but the Spirit. The Lord's Supper makes sense only after Pentecost. We must emphasize that the full experience of the Spirit in our lives is known, in part, through our celebration of the Lord's Supper. Baptism and the Lord's Supper are given to us precisely and specifically so that we can receive the gift of Pentecost and walk in the Spirit, thereby knowing the joy and blessing of the Spirit in our relationships and our work. The grace received in the Lord's Supper is the grace that is sought when we pray for Christ to fill us afresh with the Spirit.

Thus, we need to emphasize that the celebration of the Lord's Supper begins and ends with the *epiclesis*—the prayer of the church that the Spirit would be with us and infuse our worship and, in particular, our celebration of the Lord's Supper. Every dimension of meaning makes sense only in light of the Spirit's ministry. Remembrance—*anamnesis*—is not, in the end, our conjuring up as best we can a *past* event; it is, rather, a memorial in which the Spirit enables us to encounter the risen Christ today, in light of the past event.

Communion is specifically a fellowship with Christ and one another that is made possible through the gracious work of the Spirit. The Spirit brings us into fellowship with the risen Christ, and it is the unity of the Spirit, in the bond of peace, that we both celebrate and maintain when we eat together. Our experience of forgiveness—the love of God manifested in our experience of healing—is also a gift of the Spirit. The call to covenant renewal and the empowerment that comes through the nourishment of Christ's body made available to us as living bread is, again, the work of the Spirit in our lives. Much the same could be said for anticipation and Eucharist.

In other words, the continuation of Pentecost in the life and witness of the church is made possible through the celebration of the Lord's Supper. Thus, the *epiclesis* is not so much that the Spirit would be present in the elements as that the Spirit would descend on us as a people who gather for Word and sacrament. The prayer for the coming of the Spirit, therefore, belongs as much at the beginning of worship as at the end—at the beginning as we come to the ministry of the Word and of the table, and at the end as we make the transition back into the world. The gift of the Spirit in worship and particularly in the Lord's Supper is, then, a foretaste or a downpayment of the life of the Spirit that we will know in the kingdom that is yet to come.[9]

The efficacy of this event, therefore, rests not on our work or even on our faith but on the gracious work of the Spirit. This does not discount the importance of faith or of human activity. Our response to the call of Christ matters; our obedience matters; our acts of presentation and thanksgiving matter. It matters terribly that we resolve to be one people, seeking peace with one another and agreeing together that as God enables we will live

---

9. I am indebted for much of this emphasis on the place of the Spirit in the understanding of the Lord's Supper to the insights of Veli-Matti Kärkkäinen in his unpublished paper "Spirit and Supper: On the Pneumatological Understanding of the Lord's Supper," and to Leanne Van Dyk in her unpublished Regent College Summer School 2000 lecture, "The Gifts of God for the People of God."

in light of the kingdom. But the efficacy of the Lord's Supper does not, finally, rest on our faith or our sincerity or the depth of our resolve. The energy that sustains this meal and makes it a holy meal is that which is provided through the ministry of the Spirit.[10]

The Mystery of the Holy Meal and of the People of God

This leads me to conclude with two observations: This is an event of mystery, and this is an event in which we are formed as the people of God.

The affirmation of the vital ministry of the Spirit in this holy meal is a reminder that this is an event of great mystery. In this connection, I find helpful the observations of Robert Coles in his consideration of the life of Simone Weil and the caution to academics and intellectuals when it comes to such matters as the Lord's Supper. We must be careful lest we reduce the holy meal to nothing more than what can be grasped with the mind. Coles writes:

> No matter the intensity of her religious contemplation, Simone Weil was always watchful for the intrusions of the intellect. In her New York notebooks she remarks on those who can be found "reducing the bread and wine of the Eucharist to a mere symbol." She is aware how tempting such an interpretation is for so-called Christian intellectuals. But she will have no part of all that: "The mysteries then cease to be an object of contemplation; they are no longer of any use. This is the case of the illegitimate use of intelligence, and one may think that the soul of those who entertain these speculations has not yet been illumined by supernatural love."[11]

---

10. I follow Calvin at this point in believing that this does not mean that our fellowship is *only* with the Spirit. We can, with Calvin, acknowledge that Christ remains in heaven at the right hand of God—in Calvin, there is a high theology of the ascension—but that through the ministry of the Spirit we nevertheless have real communion with Christ and in the Lord's Supper participate in Christ and are fed by Christ, while also insisting that it is a nourishment made possible through the ministry of the Spirit.

11. Robert Coles, *Simone Weil: A Modern Pilgrimage* (Woodstock, VT: Skylight Paths Publishing, 2001), 145. This observation regarding Simone Weil is all the

Surely the role of theology is precisely this—to profile and protect the mystery. Surely a study such as this one, which intends to explicate the meaning of the Lord's Supper, is not meant to explain the mystery but rather to heighten our appreciation of the mystery. Furthermore, our participation in the Lord's Supper is not linked to our level of understanding or our capacity to explain the meaning of this meal. In the end, our participation is not a matter of understanding or rational comprehension but of obedience. As Thomas à Kempis reminds his readers in *The Imitation of Christ*, "God is able to work more than one can understand."[12]

I have spent the bulk of my professional life in academic circles and have often been impressed with serious, intelligent students who claim to be Christians. But when baptism comes up for discussion, some insist that they do not need it and explain why it is of little consequence. It is as though as rational people they only do what they understand and have rationally assessed they "need." The reminder of à Kempis is a good one, for both baptism and the Lord's Supper. Our approach to such an event should be one of childlike meekness before a mystery we will never fully understand. We should come with an informed obedience, certainly. But a humble obedience should always be the primary posture of heart with which we come to the mystery of the holy table.

For me, the hymn that so effectively captures the sense of wonder in this mystery is "Let All Mortal Flesh Keep Silence" from the sixth-century liturgy of St. James. The second verse brings the worshiper into an appreciative awe of the incarnation and then the Lord's Supper. It reads:

> King of Kings, yet born of woman,
> As of old on earth he stood,

---

more forcible because she was an extraordinary thinker, a first-class intellectual. But in her own coming to faith, one of the more significant turning points in her conversion was that of experiencing the mystery of God's love at the celebration of the Eucharist in Solesmes, a Benedictine abbey in northeastern France, an experience that was given more meaning for her by a poem by George Herbert that reads, "Love bade me welcome . . . drew me nearer, sweetly questioning / If I lack'd any thing."

12. Thomas à Kempis, *The Imitation of Christ*, trans. George F. Maine (London: Collins, 1957), 274 (book 4, chap. 18).

Lord of Lords, in human vesture—
In the body and the blood—
He will give to all the faithful,
His own self for heavenly food.[13]

Then the hymn proceeds to celebrate the witness of the host of heaven and the ultimate triumph over the powers of hell and the forces of darkness.

The second observation arises out of an appreciation of the central dynamic that the Spirit plays in the celebration of the Lord's Supper. By the Spirit, this meal enables the people of God to be who they are called to be. Together with the Word and prayer, this holy meal is the event that forms the people of God as a people. One of the recurring dangers within the church is that congregational life is viewed as little more than a social club with no spiritual dynamic or becomes little more than someone's project—usually the project of leaders who have an agenda they hope to accomplish, something that through their programming and strategic plans will lead to a predefined outcome, usually a larger ecclesiastical institution. While strategies and programs are certainly important, they do not constitute the essence of congregational life. Further, it is all too easy for the people to feel as though *they* are no more than a project. It is the Lord's Supper (together with the Word and prayer) that forms, reforms, and transforms people and enables them to be, specifically, the people of God. The Lord's Supper makes the church the church.

The Gospel of Luke concludes with a dramatic encounter between Jesus and two of his followers on the road to Emmaus. First, Jesus explains the Scriptures, and we read that their hearts burned within them. Then, second, they recognized him in the breaking of the bread. We might think that the church would, following this example, affirm that both the exposition of Scripture and the breaking of bread are vital to an encounter with the ascended Christ—Word and sacrament. But in most cases, church traditions have emphasized the one over against the other. Some emphasize preaching and the personal, interior response

13. "Let All Mortal Flesh Keep Silence," trans. from the liturgy of St. James by Gerard Moultrie.

to Scripture. Some, in contrast, make the focal point of worship the ceremonial, sacramental side of the faith. Yet in recent years, there has been a growing movement to bring them back together, to recover a Christian worship of two acts, two movements. The Christian community gathers first in the fellowship of the Word, to hear and receive the Word, and second at the table.

This book has given attention to the second act, not as a neglect of the first—the ministry of the Word—but as a call to appreciate more fully why the second act is the necessary complement to the first. The Lord's Supper is the meal of the church and, together with the Word and prayer, the event that enables the community of faith to be a dynamic living body, drawing energy and grace from the fountainhead of life, Jesus Christ.

SCRIPTURE INDEX